Mothers are stressed and anxious, co[...] a good enough job. We tell ourselve[...] expectations of ourselves. This makes [...] order to help ourselves. This is exactly [...] in this book. She pinpoints the source of our misery and gives us practical ways to make wonderful changes. If you want to enjoy motherhood again and lower your stress level, read this book. Among the pages you will find a wonderful transformation.

Meg Meeker, MD, author of the national bestseller
Strong Fathers, Strong Daughters

In *Remaining You While Raising Them*, Alli Worthington has given us a fresh look at what it really takes to be a good parent. With wisdom, humor, and compassion, she dispels exhausting and unhelpful motherhood myths and shows us that the best way to mother our children is to first learn how to mother ourselves.

Dr. Alison Cook, therapist and author of
The Best of You and *Boundaries for Your Soul*

There's not a mom alive who doesn't need this book. *Remaining You While Raising Them* is a true one-stop-shop manual for the mom who wants to love her kids well but needs to love herself a bit better. Thanks, Alli Worthington, for giving us real help to take the pressure off.

Lisa Whittle, bestselling author, podcast host, and speaker

Yes please. This book is *exactly* what I've been looking for as a new mom. Alli's words have inspired me to ditch old ways of thinking and embrace my style of motherhood while cheering on others who are doing the same. I'm tearing through this book, highlighting things, texting quotes to my friends, and writing Alli's reminders on the back of my hand. Alli, thank you for this.

Stephanie May Wilson, author and host of the *Girls Night* podcast

My one complaint about this book is that Alli didn't write it sooner. I had to go through the hard-fought journey of mothering four boys to gain some of these truths. You have the gift of Alli's wisdom and her excellent research to guide you in healthy mothering. Her help comes in a consumable, mom-friendly way. These chapters are relatable, to the point, and easy to grasp.

Heather MacFadyen, host of the *Don't Mom Alone*
podcast and author of *Right Where You Belong*

If you're a mom who can't remember who she was before motherhood, get this book now! *Remaining You While Raising Them* is an encouragement for any mom who wants to feel confident and fulfilled in not just her parenting but her own life too.

Christy Wright, author of *Business Boutique*,
Living True, and *Take Back Your Time*

This is the book I needed when I first became a mom, and it's the one I will keep revisiting for many years. If you're looking for a new narrative surrounding motherhood, you'll find it here. Alli speaks from a place of hard-earned experience, yet her voice is full of compassion and encouragement that we, as mamas, need. I can't wait to see the thousands of moms stepping into a place of thriving and freedom as they apply the wisdom within these pages.

Hannah Brencher, author of *Fighting Forward* and *Come Matter Here*

As a young mom, I constantly feel crushed by advice. There is always more I could be doing, as social media is ever ready to remind me. For moms of this generation, shame looms large, so when I first opened this book, I was nervous. Thankfully, my fears were instantly relieved. This book is *good news* for mothers. It is a lighter way to parenting with impact. With her signature wisdom and humor, Alli offers herself as the most generous mentor. I so enjoyed reading this book, and you will too!

Sharon Hodde Miller, author of *The Cost of Control*

From the moment I opened this book, my heart felt a huge relief and a big dose of encouragement. Alli has such a way with words—she makes you laugh, she's relatable, and she shares wise truths in a gentle but firm way. If you've ever felt like you're failing your kids or that you just don't have what it takes to do this motherhood thing well, *Remaining You While Raising Them* is just the book you need to feel less alone and be infused with practical truth and inspiration to keep on keeping on.

Crystal Paine, *New York Times* bestselling author, host of *The Crystal Paine Show*, and founder of MoneySavingMom.com

I'm a stepmom of two, and the expectations—from not only others but also myself—were crippling. Before Alli wrote this book, she coached me on balancing work, family, and purpose, all while modeling being a great mom. She lived out the principles in this book and now is sharing them to bring freedom to women. I'm grateful for this resource that will help others in the way she's helped me.

Bianca Juárez Olthoff, pastor, host of the *We're Going There* podcast, and bestselling author of *How To Have Your Life Not Suck*

REMAINING
YOU
WHILE RAISING
THEM

REMAINING YOU WHILE RAISING THEM

The Secret Art of Confident Motherhood

ALLI WORTHINGTON

ZONDERVAN
BOOKS

ZONDERVAN BOOKS

Remaining You While Raising Them
Copyright © 2023 by Alli Worthington

Requests for information should be addressed to:
Zondervan, *3900 Sparks Dr. SE, Grand Rapids, Michigan 49546*

Zondervan titles may be purchased in bulk for educational, business, fundraising, or sales
promotional use. For information, please email SpecialMarkets@Zondervan.com.

ISBN 978-0-310-35879-4 (softcover)
ISBN 978-0-310-35881-7 (audio)
ISBN 978-0-310-35880-0 (ebook)

Author is represented by Jenni Burke of Illuminate Literary Agency, www.illuminateliterary.com.

Cover design: Faceout Studio
Cover illustrations: Marish / GoodStudio / Shutterstock
Interior illustrations: Jenna Burns
Interior design: Denise Froehlich

Printed in the United States of America

23 24 25 26 27 LBC 5 4 3 2 1

For my children,
my greatest joy this
side of heaven

Contents

PART 1

Modern Motherhood Is Broken

We haven't met yet, but I bet we have more in common than not. I know you want to be a wonderful mother. Whether you arrived at motherhood by birth, adoption, or marriage, you want to get it right.

Perhaps motherhood is way harder than you expected. You worry that you aren't doing enough or that you're doing too much. Mom guilt is a constant one-thousand-pound weight on your shoulders. It seems there's no escaping it. You also feel lonely, but at the same time, you long for some time alone. It's as though there aren't enough hours in the day to squeeze in time to yourself that is fulfilling.

I also know motherhood has shown you that you are stronger than you knew. You've learned you are capable of deep sacrificial love. I know because I've been a mother for the last two decades and have talked to thousands of other mothers too.

I promise that by the end of our time together, you will have new wisdom, more confidence, and a full toolbox. In part 1, let's dive into the problem with modern motherhood.

CHAPTER 1

Modern Motherhood Is Broken, and It's Breaking Us

On a crisp September day, our new neighbors pulled into the driveway next door with their moving truck. I took a sip of my coffee and watched them from my backyard deck, chuckling to myself. *Well, I guess we didn't scare them off.*

Three weeks earlier, I had seen them viewing the home for sale. They were a charming middle-aged couple, holding hands as they walked toward the open front door of the home. They looked so sweet, so unsuspecting, so . . . normal.

I rounded up all five of my sons and commanded them to go outside. "Go run around the backyard," I said. "And make lots and lots of noise." The lovely couple deserved a fair warning about who they would live next to if they bought that house.

The kids swung lightsabers, played football, and ran in circles, wildly making random noises as only a group of five boys can do. The real estate agent gave me a wicked side-eye as she hurried the couple into the house. Mission accomplished.

No one deserves to buy a home with five boys next door without a proper heads-up. I'm not a monster.

As the new neighbors unloaded their truck, I saw the woman in the backyard and went out to greet her. "You came back!" I yelled out as I walked her way. "All these boys didn't scare you away?"

"Oh, no, honey. I raised three myself. Nothing I haven't seen . . ." Her words trailed off in confusion as amusement washed over her face.

I turned to see my three-year-old toddling down the brick stairs. His right hand holding the rail, his feet cushioned by bright blue Crocs, and wearing nothing else, he yelled out the cutest little "Hello!" *Bless it all.*

I'd love to tell you things like that didn't happen around my house very often. But with five boys, one stepdaughter, a pampered golden retriever, and a slew of random pets, I have learned to roll with what each day brings.

Can I be honest? Before I had kids, I always imagined I would be a great mom. It was equal parts ignorance and excitement. I told my now husband on a blind date that I wanted five children. I'm still amazed he didn't run away, leaving a man-shaped hole in the restaurant wall. Nope, he was down for all of it. We both were.

We had it all worked out. We knew exactly what kind of parents we were going to be. Of course, we're all experts before we have kids, right?

I had no idea motherhood would be my greatest joy and also the hardest thing I would ever do. I wasn't prepared for how motherhood would change my life, and I certainly wasn't prepared for how it would change me.

Physically, my body has never been the same. I've been tired now for twenty-four years, and I'm still searching for the perfect concealer to hide it. Contrary to my hopes, I did not roll out of the hospital in my prepregnancy jeans, and I've been way fluffier ever since. I finally made peace with the stretch marks, but I do still wish spray tans worked on them. After every spray tan, I look a bit like a tiger. And trampolines still make me pee even if I haven't had water in two days. I must have a reserve just waiting for me to start jumping.

Spiritually, motherhood brought me closer to God. I saw how I loved my firstborn. No matter how much of a tiny tyrant he was, my love for him was endless. It was a fierce, protective love that would make me fight a bear blindfolded with a butter knife if need be. I no longer wondered how God could love me so much. It made sense that God loved me with that same protective passion.

What no one warned me about was the emotional toll of motherhood. Not a single person, book, magazine, or article warned me that motherhood would require raising my children *and* raising myself. No one told me that as my kids changed and developed, so would I.

I knew about the joy and excitement motherhood would bring. And I had some clue about the exhaustion, both physical and mental. But I didn't know exhaustion could be followed by guilt, shame, and resentment if I didn't learn to care for myself.

You Aren't the Only One

Being a mother is the most wonderful, life-changing, fulfilling job in the world. But it's also the most challenging, exhausting, leave-you-wanting-to-suck-your-thumb-in-a-corner experience too. Both of those things are solid truth, existing together in the same space.

Motherhood is like winning the lottery and working a nightmare job at the same time.

It gives me purpose, and yet some days I feel lost and lonely.

Being a mom is both rewarding and somehow also annoying.

It gives life meaning, but also, why does there have to be so much poop?

We enter motherhood with crazy-high expectations and don't for one second think they are unrealistic. Mostly, these expectations aren't of our own making. They are thrust upon us by our friends, our coworkers, our neighbors, our crazy aunt Sarah, our parents and grandparents, and worst of all, social media.

Motherhood is the ultimate both/and endurance challenge.

Between the parenting books, the baby showers, and—heaven help us—the perfect gender reveal party, we start motherhood overwhelmed. We imagine cute newborn photo shoots where our babies don't cry and where we look like models just a few weeks after giving birth. We see ourselves jumping back into our regular work schedules and routines without missing a beat or a board meeting. We imagine that in motherhood we'll feel a lot like we felt before we had children—only happier.

But motherhood is harder, messier, crazier, and more amazing than anything we could have imagined.

Being a mother brings deep joy and meaning to life. The love we have for our kids is all-consuming and transformative. We aren't who we used to be. We are somehow changed in the most exquisite and inexplicable ways. We are more resilient, loving, and complex versions of our old selves.

But there's also this other thing that happens in motherhood. Deep down, we have the unsettled feeling we are somehow getting it wrong. It happens in the day-to-day, when we feel like we may never be ourselves again, somehow drowning in diapers, dinners, and the desires of others. We ask ourselves, "Why can't I get it together?"

We look on social media and see all the other moms doing it

well. Those moms have their ducks in a row. Meanwhile, we don't even have ducks. We have squirrels, and they are at a rave. "It must just be me," we think. Somehow we didn't get the secret motherhood memo telling us how to balance everything while also enjoying every moment and feeling great about ourselves and our kids.

We don't know what we're doing wrong or how to fix it. And we don't know what to do with how we feel. But don't worry, you aren't the only one.

Mom Guilt—The Shame We Share

Mom guilt is the crusher of our motherhood dreams. It can sneak up on us when we least expect it. It takes us out at the knees and turns us into women who have way too many conversations about how we are failing.

The lowest moment in my motherhood journey was the time I came within minutes of killing my son Jack. He was recovering from ACL reconstruction surgery after a football injury. He was forty-eight hours out of surgery and in so much pain that I stayed with him almost around the clock.

I made him a snack of pesto sauce on noodles—classic comfort food for a miserable, well-medicated boy. A few minutes after he ate, he said, "Mom, my throat is getting sore."

In a seven-person household, someone is always coming down with something, so his statement didn't really register. A few minutes later, Jack said, "Wow, my skin is itchy. Look at this rash." *Red splotches? Sore throat? What in the world?*

I called my cousin, an emergency room physician, thinking Jack was reacting to his pain medicine. She immediately asked about food and guessed he was allergic to something he ate. He has a peanut allergy, but I'm a hawk about it. He never gets near peanuts. I knew that wasn't it. But then what was it?

Surely it wasn't the pesto. He ate pesto all the time. But then I remembered it was a new brand. I ran to check the label. It didn't have peanuts, but it did have cashews in it. Was he allergic to cashews? *Who puts cashews in pesto?*

I couldn't find Jack's EpiPen, so I gave him liquid Benadryl and decided to race him to the ER myself because I could get there in four minutes flat. I didn't trust an ambulance to get him to the hospital faster than I could get him there myself. What if the ambulance was out helping other people? What if they said it would be a fifteen-minute wait? What if . . . what if . . .

My husband, Mark, carried Jack to the minivan and angled his lanky frame into the back seat to avoid bending his postsurgery leg. Once he was locked and loaded, I drove that minivan like a NASCAR driver, scream-asking him if he was OK every thirty seconds. Slamming on the brakes outside the ER, I ran through the double doors and burst into panicked tears. I screamed, "Help me! I need help! Somebody help me!"

A few minutes later, Jack was safely hooked to an IV in the ER, sleeping off the anaphylaxis. I sat next to him, weeping in a little metal chair, my internal monologue thrashing me for my carelessness. *How could you be so thoughtless? Of all the stupid things. I mean, you didn't even know where his EpiPen was! You almost killed your own son.* It broke me.

My guilt convinced me that I was a terrible mother. For months, the guilt of that day stuck with me like a knife in my side. I woke up with nightmares about losing him. I couldn't shake the guilt.

When he woke up Jack laughed about how we had learned he was allergic to cashews. Years later, he still teases me about the time I "tried to kill him." It's a joke in our family to this day, but even though I laugh, it still stings a bit.

You may not have accidentally almost pesto-poisoned your

kid like I did, but I bet you wrestle with your own mom guilt. How do I know?

Along with our fierce love for our children, the one thing that bonds all moms together is guilt. Soul-crushing, happiness-stealing mom guilt. Mom guilt is the extra gift of motherhood we didn't ask for or want. It tells us we aren't doing enough, we aren't doing it right, and we're totally messing up our kids in the process.

Our love for our children makes us vulnerable to guilt, regret, and anxiety, which causes us to second-guess the decisions we make. Though these feelings come from a place of good intentions, a place of love and hope, they come out as a weapon that wounds us again and again.

Mom-Guilt Triggers

Without warning, mom guilt comes crashing into our internal monologue, stealing our joy and crushing our souls. The worst part about mom guilt is we sometimes don't know who or what will trigger it. But there are some common triggers.

Do these sound familiar?

THE GRANDMA GUILT BOMBER

Grandmas, whether our own mom or our mother-in-law, have a way of triggering our mom guilt. If there's anyone we want to prove our supermom skills to, it's them. So when they say, "I just love how you guys don't worry about putting the boys to bed dirty. Y'all are so much more relaxed than we were!" we hear, "I can't believe you don't make your kids take a bath before bed!" When they say, "It's great you don't force your kids to eat foods they don't like," we hear, "You aren't feeding your kids the foods they need to be healthy."

One well-meaning comment can be all it takes to send us into a spiral of shame.

THE HUSBAND HASSLE

Of all the husband hassles that cause immediate mom guilt (and possibly a little anger), the question "What'd you do all day?" is one of the worst. He might genuinely be asking about your day. But your mom guilt convinces you he's saying you must have spent your day lying around, watching the kids redecorate the house with toys and trash while you ate chocolate-covered strawberries and watched rom-coms.

THE FRIEND FAIL

We all need friends who speak the truth in love, but sometimes even our friends trigger our guilt. One time my friend texted me to remind me it was picture day. She didn't want me to be embarrassed like the year before when I sent my youngest to school in an old *Blue's*

Clues shirt for picture day. She wasn't trying to trigger my guilt. But she did.

Once our mom guilt is triggered, it tears us down over imagined failures and convinces us we will never get it right.

When I asked friends what triggered their mom guilt in the past week, I heard the following:

- Yelling at my kids.
- Having to work so much as a single mom.
- Not having enough money for what she wants.
- Letting them watch TV.
- Allowing too much video game time.
- He's having friend trouble. Did I not prepare him enough? Did I do too much?
- I didn't read to her enough when she was young. Is that why her grades are bad now?
- Seeing what other families are doing kills me.
- Am I being selfish for chasing my dream?

Mom guilt and the feeling that we're failing seem to be the default for modern moms.

Maybe you've felt it too. I know I have.

In a Barna study, 95 percent of mothers said they want to do better in at least one area of their lives. Let me clarify that for us—*95 percent of mothers feel like they are failing in at least one area.* Not only that, but

- 80 percent say they are stressed out,
- 70 percent say they are tired,
- 62 percent say they are dissatisfied with their work/life balance, and
- 56 percent say they are overcommitted.[1]

In my own nationwide survey of more than one thousand women, 65 percent of women said motherhood is way harder than they thought it would be. And 96 percent said mom guilt is something they struggle with.

What surprised me most was that social media was the number one trigger for mom guilt. Yes, more than our grandmas, our husbands, or our close friends, social media was the most triggering of all.

You've been there: You're having a great day. Life feels manageable. The kids are calm, and you have a few minutes to yourself. You open your phone to see what's happening, and there's *that mom*. You know the one: She's always calm and put together. Her kids are happy and well-behaved. Never once has an empty food wrapper fallen out of her car in the school drop-off line. She has posted a picture of her family laughing as they stand over a flawlessly clean kitchen island. Even her ridiculously good-looking dog is smiling. Meanwhile, you're wearing yesterday's clothes, your hair is in a weird bun with enough dry shampoo in it to soak up an oil spill, and your kitchen doesn't have a single countertop that isn't covered in a pile of papers or half-eaten sandwiches. Immediately, you hate your life.

You tell yourself that your family deserves better than this. Guilt washes over you faster than you can throw your phone across the room, and you yell, "Why is our dog so dirty?" As if the dog is what you're actually upset about.

What we see when we scroll through our newsfeed confirms our most annoyingly persistent thought: "Other moms are getting it right. Why can't I?"

How in the world did we get here? Motherhood is amazing. It's meant to be incredible, life-changing, invigorating, centering, and all the other happy words we can think of.

And it is . . . except when it isn't.

And it's the "isn't" part that I want to pull us into for a closer look.

It's time we all face reality: **modern motherhood is broken, and it's breaking us.**

Even as I write that sentence, I feel the weight and truth of it in my soul.

Maybe you feel it too. Many of us are collapsing under the invisible pressure that motherhood brings. Yet we've convinced ourselves we are the only ones who feel it.

My friend Jennifer, an accountant and mother of three, shared what many of us feel.

Modern motherhood may be broken, but we don't have to let it break us anymore.

> I'm exhausted. I love my kids with every ounce of me, but I feel so much disappointment at myself for not doing a better job. From the moment I open my eyes in the morning until I crawl into bed at night, I'm always behind. There's never enough time and not enough of me to go around. This isn't what I thought motherhood would be. What am I doing wrong? I need someone to tell me what I'm doing wrong before I ruin my kids completely.

We all want to raise healthy kids and give them every opportunity to have a great life. But what if we've been so focused on all the other "hoods" (toddlerhood, childhood, teenagehood) that we've forgotten the "mother" in motherhood?

What if raising incredible, emotionally healthy kids begins with paying attention to our emotional health?

Modern motherhood is broken, but you don't have to let it break you anymore. You can remain you while raising them. You can thrive while raising them. The answer is found in the secret art to confident motherhood.

I Want You to Remember

At the end of each chapter, I'm including a few key takeaways to remember, discussion questions to answer, and action steps to help you remain you while raising them. Grab a journal and maybe a small group of friends, and let's dive in together.

Motherhood is the ultimate both/and endurance challenge. Being a mother is the most wonderful, life-changing, fulfilling job in the world. But it's also the most challenging, exhausting, leave-you-wanting-to-suck-your-thumb-in-a-corner experience too.

Our love for our children makes us vulnerable to guilt, regret, and anxiety, which causes us to second-guess the decisions we make. Though these feelings come from a place of good intentions, a place of love and hope, they come out as a weapon that wounds us again and again.

Social media is the biggest single cause of mom guilt. You open your phone and, boom, you get triggered and feel certain you are the worst mom ever. What we see when we scroll through our newsfeed confirms our most annoyingly persistent thought: "Other moms are getting it right. Why can't I?"

Modern motherhood may be broken, but we don't have to let it break us anymore.

Journal and Discussion

♥ What parts of motherhood have you experienced as a both/and challenge?

♥ Which of the mom-guilt triggers resonate with you?

♥ How has social media triggered you?

♥ Have you experienced a deep worry that you are getting mothering wrong?

CHAPTER 2

If Mama Ain't Happy

My boys were five, three, and a baby when I walked into my mother-in-law's kitchen. There was Anna, up early, making a big breakfast, chatting with them as though talking to toddlers was the most exciting part of her day.

My stepdaughter, Jessica, was with us as well, and Anna was equally engaged with her, chatting about the latest craze in the world of eight-year-olds.

I stood there for a moment and watched her in awe. She was everything I thought I would be as a mom. She was happy, energetic, playful, all while whipping up a great meal. I had planned to be that mom—happy, calm, doing all the things. I just knew I'd be a modern-day Mary Poppins. I'd take care of business with a smile on my face, and then we'd have adventures and make memories.

I sat down at her table with a long, slow sigh. She looked up from the pancake she was flipping, turned her head just a bit, and raised an eyebrow in response to my sigh.

"I don't know how you do it. I saw this whole mom-life thing going way differently than it is. I always wanted to be a mom like you are. But I'm not. I'm tired, I'm grumpy, and I yell all the time. I'm not a happy, carefree mom. I'm not Mary Poppins at all!"

Anna put down her spatula and wiped her hands on a yellow towel, shaking her head as she chuckled in a half whisper, "Mary Poppins."

Anna had my full attention. She explained that she wasn't happy and calm when her kids were little. She was like this now only because she wasn't parenting littles. It was easier to be a part-time grandma than a full-time mom. She promised me it would get easier.

I couldn't imagine it getting easier. My older boys never stopped wrestling (at least not until one of them was bleeding), and the baby wouldn't relax unless I was holding him. I dreamed of using the bathroom without an audience or sipping a drink without having to share it. I wanted to be left alone for five seconds without worrying that my little guys would hurt themselves, hurt each other, or destroy the house. And I felt guilty for wanting to be left alone.

Although I loved being a mom, I found mothering to be both physically overstimulating and intellectually boring. The constant stress of motherhood and the physical exhaustion of caring for young kids left me feeling lonely and miserable. I was emotionally burned out.

> Motherhood can be both physically overstimulating and intellectually boring.

Motherhood was too much and yet, at the same time, not enough. That left me feeling like I was too much and yet somehow also not enough. It was a constant mental tug-of-war, and it was breaking me. And I wasn't alone in the battle.

Vanessa, a good friend of mine, shared her similar struggle. She believed that how her kids turned out in life depended solely on how well she did her job as a mom. She believed that nothing else in her life was more important than getting motherhood 100 percent right. She believed that if her kids failed, it was because she didn't help them enough. If they didn't excel academically or athletically, it was because she didn't give them the right resources. If their health was poor, it was because she didn't feed them organically grown, locally sourced, grass-fed, cage-free, free-range meals.

At the end of each day, she fell into bed exhausted and defeated with a long list of ways she hadn't measured up. She told me she was constantly yelling, always tired, forever overwhelmed, always in a hurry, and always in a bad mood. Her expectations were so high that the weight of them was crushing her.

She said, "I was actually failing my kids by trying to be everything for them. I knew something had to change, and that something was me. I wasn't going to be a better mom by doing more for my kids; I was going to be a better mom by being a better me."

Vanessa's words were comforting. I didn't have to do more to be a better mom. I just had to be a better me. But as I thought about her words, the first toddler meltdown of the day unfolded in front of me, and I reacted. Once again I told myself I was a bad mom. Tired, lazy, and grumpy were the words I used to describe myself. I wasn't the magic-carpetbag-carrying, spoon-full-of-sugar mom I imagined I would be. I went through the motions, believing I was a lousy mom who was messing up her kids. I put myself, my needs, and my happiness on the shelf and trudged through life every day.

A few months later, I was visiting my friend Laura. As our seven kids destroyed her living room, I tearfully confessed, "Laura, I'm afraid I might be a terrible mother."

She listened as I laid out the evidence I had against myself, then she told me what I needed to hear—the truth. Laura is a brilliant counselor who doesn't pull punches, even with her friends. She reminded me that Mary Poppins was the nanny, not the mama, so of course she was always singing and dancing and having fun and playing games. The woman was sleeping at night. And she probably had the weekends off. She wasn't the mama, the wife, the budget maker, the grocery shopper, and the cook while also running a business.

"Being the nanny was her business, Alli, it wasn't her life. Girl, you need to get over that expectation right now."

I had to wrap my head around the truth that being a good mom isn't based on some imaginary Disney-level happiness or all the things I do for my kids. If I were to take anything from Mary Poppins's example, maybe I should be kind to myself. Get some rest. Take some time off. Discover what I enjoy doing *without* my kids.

What if being the best mother I could be meant I had to start by mothering myself?

Laura shared that we moms are often so focused on our kids' well-being that we neglect our own. When we neglect ourselves long enough, we become emotionally unhealthy. And when we mother from an unhealthy place long enough, we raise emotionally unhealthy children. Mothering yourself means taking care of your needs just like you take care of the needs of your children.

Being the best mother you can be starts with learning to mother yourself.

Here were three women, moms I greatly respected, all saying the same thing. I had focused my expectations on what I did as a mom, not who I was as a mother.

That day I began asking myself this one question: What if motherhood isn't about what I do but who I am? How different would my life (and my parenting) be if I invested in my relational, emotional, mental, physical, and spiritual health?

If Mama Ain't Happy

Experts say emotional health is how you think and feel, how emotionally intelligent you are, and how well you can regulate your emotions.[1] But as a nonprofessional, I believe emotional health is a combination of spiritual, mental, and relational health.

I want my kids to love God, have a positive outlook on life, be in great relationships, and know how to give and receive love. I pray they have firm boundaries, take personal responsibility for themselves, and enjoy a great life. That's my description of an emotionally healthy life. Who doesn't want this for their kids?

If we can raise our kids to be emotionally healthy adults, we'll have hit the jackpot as moms, right?

But I don't want an emotionally healthy life just for my kids, I also want that life for myself. I want to love God, have a positive outlook on life, be in great relationships, and know how to give and receive love. I hope to maintain wise boundaries, take personal responsibility for myself, and enjoy a life well-lived.

In my twenty-four years as a mom, I have waded through countless parenting books, sought the expertise of counselors, coached thousands of women in my programs, and sifted through mountains of my own research only to discover this shocking truth: **the greatest gift I can give my kids is to be an emotionally healthy mom and to model the way for them.**

But how do we get there when motherhood feels so broken?

The answer is closer than we think.

I have a friend who is an older mom. She raised two children to adulthood and then, in her fifties, adopted two toddlers. People often ask her if she is a better mom the second time around, and

EMOTIONAL HEALTH IS A COMBINATION OF SPIRITUAL, MENTAL, AND RELATIONAL HEALTH.

she answers with a resounding and confident yes every time. People usually follow up with, "Is it because you know more about parenting?" To which she replies, "No, it's because I know more about myself."

From the moment we learn we are going to be a mother, whether by birth, adoption, or marriage, our focus shifts from our needs to the needs of our child. Books we read, podcasts we listen to, and social media posts we see fill our minds with what we must do to care for that little one.

As they grow, we spend less time on their physical needs and instead attend to their overall development.

> The greatest gift you can give your kids is to be an emotionally healthy mom and to model the way for them.

We want them to discover who they are, what they love, and who they will become. But along the way, we stop attending to our own development, our own activities, our own needs. We get lost in the shuffle.

We know motherhood has changed us; how can it not? But we don't take the time to discover and develop this new version of ourselves because we don't feel we have the time or the right. We think the many other pressing needs have to be met before we take the time to get to know this new woman we see in the mirror. And the farther she gets pushed out of the way, the more lost she feels.

Claire, a coaching client of mine who is an entrepreneur who works from home, recently shared,

> Becoming a mother was all-consuming for me. I knew every-
> thing about pregnancy. I decorated the nursery, and I had a
> plan for everything. I took care of every need and had a backup
> plan for every surprise that could pop up. I was . . . I mean, I
> am a great mom. But after a few years, I wound up depressed,

23

lonely, and I guess . . . bitter. I loved my daughter desperately, but I forgot how to care for myself. *In becoming a mother, I abandoned myself.*

You may feel like you have abandoned yourself in your motherhood journey too. So many mothers do. Together, we'll unpack how to care for yourself well because taking care of yourself is just as important as taking care of your child. As much as you learn to anticipate their needs, you have to stay connected to your own. As much as you carefully attend to their development, you must keep developing and investing in yourself.

I'm sure you have heard the saying "If Mama ain't happy, ain't nobody happy." And while it's a fun saying, it carries deep truth. If we want our children to be happy, confident, and emotionally steady with healthy boundaries, we must live that way ourselves. A mother's emotional health (her spiritual, mental, and relational health) is the most important legacy she can give her children.

The healthier you are, the healthier and happier your kids are likely to be.

Our culture teaches us that for our kids to be well, we have to focus solely on their development and happiness. But in doing so, we push ourselves and our emotional health so far into the background that we lose ourselves.

The more a mother sacrifices and puts herself last, the more likely she is to teach her children to do the same. Her daughters believe the same myths, perpetuating the cycle of what we now know to be broken modern motherhood, and her sons grow up believing they'll have that kind of wife and mother to their kids, for better or worse.

A MOTHER'S EMOTIONAL HEALTH IS THE MOST IMPORTANT LEGACY SHE CAN GIVE HER CHILDREN.

The Gospel of Grace

Motherhood changed me, not just physically and emotionally but also spiritually. The gospel of grace was an idea that sounded good in theory, but I could never fully grasp how God's love for me was unconditional. Surely there must be something I could do, some way I could fail that would finally make God wash his hands of me.

We are God's creation, his beloved. He sacrificed everything for us and gave us such perfect love that nothing could separate us from him. It wasn't until I became a mother that I fully grasped the gospel of grace, God's perfect, unconditional love for me, his child.

My friend Carol told me about how sending her oldest son to school taught her about God's love.

Alli, there was something about that milestone that was so terrifying. It sent doubts about my mothering skills into overdrive. Maybe it was because for the first time in his life, I would have the least control over how he spent his day. I was dusting his bedroom, crying and worrying that I hadn't done enough to prepare him for life outside our home. Once again, I was telling myself that if I hadn't done my job well, he wouldn't become the man God had created him to be. As I ran my fingers across his pinewood derby trophy, I felt like God said, "Carol, I love him more than you could ever imagine loving him. You are his mother, but I am his creator. I sacrificed everything for him."

As she finished her story, I realized this truth: **God has already written the future of every single one of my children.** Sure, I have to do my part as their mom, but nothing I do can ruin the future God has for them. The weight of their future is on him, not on me. In today's modern motherhood, we carry a weight that God never intended us to carry.

God extended his gospel of grace to my children as well. His love for them is also perfect. And according to his promise in Scripture, nothing—neither death nor life, neither angels nor demons, neither the present nor the future, nor any powers, neither height nor depth, nor anything else in all creation (including any shortcomings I might have as a mom)—can separate my children from the love of God in Christ Jesus (Romans 8:38–39).

Even if nothing else takes the weight of motherhood off our shoulders, that promise alone should. Amen and hallelujah.

Changing my mindset about motherhood began with understanding how God viewed my role as a mom.

Changing the Way You Think

I'm offering you a new way to think—about your kids, about yourself, about motherhood. I want to reveal the myths that have broken modern motherhood. And then I want to show you a new paradigm, a mindset that strips away the myths we have believed: myths that tell us we are doing it wrong, our work will hurt our kids, other moms have it together, and good moms should be happy all the time—just to name a few.

Together we'll debunk the myth that investing in yourself is selfish. And we will discover how becoming the healthiest mom you can be is the greatest asset to your family.

I waited until I was a parent for twenty-four years to write this book, partly because I wanted to make sure I knew what I was talking about and that my kids would turn out OK—*seriously*. But I also knew mothers needed more than another parenting book. There are a million books focused on trying to manage kids, but hardly anything for the mothers. In my survey of over one thousand mothers, I asked them to share the best book on motherhood they had ever read, and 95 percent of them named a parenting book.

You see the problem, right? We've accidentally abandoned ourselves in the process of mothering our children.

Today I'm still on the journey, just like you. I have kids from middle school to college and adulthood. I haven't forgotten the sleepless nights, because I still have them. My house is still a mess, I still can't manage to cook a big meal unless it comes out of a Crock-Pot, someone still always has someplace to be or a project due, and sometimes I still long for one day of peace and quiet. But I'm also far enough along to be able to say to you that motherhood isn't just about what you do, it's about who you are. *The mom you are is what your kids will remember.* They won't remember everything you did, but they will for sure remember who you were.

Motherhood isn't about what you do, it's about who you are.

Remaining You While Raising Them is not a parenting book; it's a book for you, about you, centered and focused entirely on you. You've been mothering without a road map, weighed down by social pressure, mom guilt, and myths that have convinced you for far too long that you're failing. And it's not your fault.

Modern motherhood may be broken, but we can change it together. And when we change ourselves for the better, our families can change for the better too.

I'm here to help you overcome losing yourself in the demands of motherhood, discover the unique type of mom you are, develop simple habits that will make your life easier, build friendships that make you happier, and learn new ways to take care of yourself in the midst of a full life.

In this book, you won't find a step-by-step plan to raise

perfect children because that, my friend, is an impossible dream. I'm not going to give you the solution to every parenting issue. Those types of books are already out there and haven't helped us out of this predicament anyway, right? It's time for something new.

Whether you are looking forward to becoming a mom through birth, adoption, or marriage; are in the throes of raising a little one or navigating the school years; or are an empty nester enjoying being a grandma, this book is for you. You will find encouragement, research-backed truths, and a guilt-free guide to embracing motherhood.

The weight of motherhood doesn't have to crush us. We can thrive as healthier, happier moms, and the secret to getting there is easier than you might think. We can learn to enjoy motherhood again.

Sure, modern motherhood may be broken. But we can rediscover the beauty, the joy, and the sacred and secret art of confident motherhood together.

I Want You to Remember

Emotional health is a combination of spiritual, mental, and relational health.

Being the best mother you can be starts with learning to mother yourself. We can be so focused on our kids' well-being that we neglect our own. When we neglect ourselves long enough, we become emotionally unhealthy. And when we mother from an unhealthy place long enough, we raise emotionally unhealthy children. Mothering yourself means taking care of your needs as well as the needs of your children.

The greatest gift you can give your kids is to be an emotionally healthy mom and to model the way for them.

The more a mother sacrifices and puts herself last, the more likely she is to teach her children to do the same. Her daughters believe the same myths, perpetuating the cycle of what we now know to be broken modern motherhood, and her sons grow up believing they'll have that kind of wife and mother to their kids, for better or worse.

Motherhood isn't about what you do, it's about who you are.

Journal and Discussion

♥ Have you ever thought about how important it is to invest in your emotional health?

♥ How does it feel to think about "mothering yourself"?

♥ How good are you at letting go of control and knowing God is in charge of your children's lives and futures? Are there certain aspects that are easier than others?

CHAPTER 3

Your Mom Superpower

A big, clunky, early 2010s digital photo frame is the most important thing in my kitchen. Given my love for kitchen appliances, you might think my beloved dishwasher or my air fryer would hold the top spot. If my stovetop burners could talk, they'd tell you that the right front burner and I have a special something-something going on.

But the digital photo frame? That's the best part of my kitchen. As of today, it holds a little over three thousand photos: our wedding, births, holidays, trips, a lot of blowing out birthday candles, and average everyday snaps from the last twenty-five years of our life. The constant scrolling of pictures will catch us, lure us in, and flood our memories. Five minutes will go by, and we'll wonder why we walked into the kitchen in the first place.

Guests love it, and extended family members can't wait to see if their photos will scroll through. The boys' friends and girl-friends (girlfriends love seeing those cute baby pictures!) have all been caught in its web of happiness.

I see the happy moments and feel the warm flood of nostalgia. Otherwise lost in the daily grind of raising kids, memories come back fresh. Sometimes I laugh, sometimes I tear up, and sometimes I cringe at what I see in the photos.

I notice how filthy and cluttered my house was for years. I laugh at how funny the boys looked in hand-me-downs they weren't quite big enough to wear. And I can't believe the clothes I let them wear out of the house. I'm also reminded why my husband forbids me from ever trying to cut their hair again to save money.

I'll confess that I've sometimes been tempted to delete some of the photos. Unlike a curated Instagram feed full of beautiful, posed family photos, my digital frame is full of real life. I see our joys, our successes, and our hard times.

It's also a highlight reel of all the ways I have failed my kids, including the first-day-of-school photos taken on the second day of school, last-minute family birthday parties thrown together, and let's not forget the preschool photo in the *Blue's Clues* shirt.

For over a decade, that photo frame was a mixed blessing. Everyone loved it. But sometimes I didn't want to look and remember how many times I had failed my kids.

One time, when my oldest was going back to college after an extended visit home, he stopped and hugged me and said, "Hey Mom, can you send me all the pictures off the photo frame?"

A few hours later, I had all the photos backed up in the cloud and sent the link around in our family group chat. Within moments he texted, "I can't stop looking at this. I love it. *It's the story of us.*" He didn't see the failures or the disappointments. He looked with fresh eyes and saw a happy family with stories, ups and downs, and above all, love.

The story of us is beautiful. Not perfect, not even always happy. Definitely not easy. But it is our story: everything we are to each other, our shared experiences, our memories, life's most precious moments, the comedies, the dramas, the time I almost killed Jack—all of it.

THE STORY OF US

As a mom, I've failed a thousand times, but I've also made a million magic moments. And I bet you have too. You've created those moments by

- reading an extra story at bedtime.
- throwing back the covers and inviting your little one into bed after a bad dream.
- encouraging your child when they got a bad grade on a spelling test.
- celebrating their success of learning to ride their bike without training wheels.
- making popcorn and snuggling up on the couch and watching a movie.
- comforting your heartbroken teen after their first breakup.

When we zoom in on what we wish were different, or moments we aren't proud of, then of course all we see is the bad. But instead of zooming in, we have to learn to zoom out and look at the big picture of the beautiful, messy, never-ever-perfect life and family God has given us.

One study showed that as moms of infants, we only have to get it right 50 percent of the time to be great moms and create a secure attachment with our kids.[1]

Secure attachment happens when a child forms a secure bond

33

with their mother. This bond enables the child to feel safe, comforted, and to trust their mother. As they grow older, children with secure attachment tend to have better social skills, form healthy relationships, and are more confident, empathetic, and able to regulate their emotions.

Secure attachment in childhood is the basis of a child being able to love others and receive love. This attachment lays the foundation for a person's ability to establish healthy and fulfilling relationships throughout their life. Luckily, creating a secure bond with our child comes naturally for most moms: we create the bond through comforting, snuggling, feeding, and providing a nurturing, safe environment.

The relief that I don't have to get it right 100 percent of the time takes the pressure off and allows me to give myself grace when I fall short. It's not a license to just throw my hands up and say, "Oh well, they'll survive!" But knowing I don't have to get it right all the time is a built-in cushion of grace given to us by God.

Moms have to get it right only 50 percent of the time to be great moms.

He knew motherhood would be hard work and made a way for mothers to survive it.

But I bet you are like me and zoom in on the mistakes, forgetting to zoom out for the big picture too. You don't even realize what a great mom you are. And like my photo frame, I bet the big picture of your life is a beautiful story too.

Have you ever noticed that it's way easier to focus on our mistakes than our successes? How crazy is it that you can live sleep-deprived (which is literally torture by the way), be on duty for tiny tyrants 24/7, have kids who have raised button-pushing to an art form, and yet be a loving, mature, well-adjusted woman at the same time? That's amazing.

I know you're a great mom. Do you know how I know? Because you are reading this book. The simple act of investing in yourself to create a happier, healthier home life is something a great mom would do.

Here's what I bet is true about you: you love your kids with a depth you never knew was possible. Like Tony Stark, you would put on the **A great mom invests in herself to create a happier, healthier home life.** glove in *Avengers: Endgame* and snap your fingers. You would jump down into the pit of snakes like Indiana Jones. And you would run across no-man's-land like Wonder Woman to protect your kids.

I also know you worry you don't do enough.

And you worry you do too much.

You feel like you don't have any time for yourself, but you keep smiling through it and pushing forward.

You feel guilty for struggling with loneliness.

You wish you didn't feel bored with the day-to-day of motherhood.

You struggle because you can't solve every problem.

You feel guilty for needing to take a break and get away.

In other words, you are a normal, healthy, amazing mom who loves her kids. You aren't alone in these feelings. All moms feel this way. I know because I've polled thousands of women about motherhood over the last three years while I researched this book for you. You'll hear stories (with names changed for privacy, of course) from many women I've coached through the years. You will see that you aren't alone.

You are spectacular and strong beyond what you give yourself credit for. Before you had kids, could you have imagined needing to clean the kitchen so many times each day? How does it get so messy?

Who knew laundry would be a never-ending battle you would have to fight daily just to stay on top of it? And why is every piece of clothing inside out? And Lord help you if you ever miss a day. Good luck ever catching up.

Would you have imagined that Cheerios would be your constant companion? In the bottom of your purse, between the couch cushions, stuck in your hair, or worse yet, stuck on the back of your pants? **Cheerios are the sad confetti of the motherhood party.**

If no one has told you lately that you are doing a great job, I'm sorry. You deserve to hear it often. Most of what you do is underappreciated and underacknowledged. Cut yourself some slack, mama. You have permission to give yourself grace. God's grace is sufficient for you and me.

> You have permission to give yourself grace. God's grace is sufficient for you and me.

Did you know that God gave every mom a unique superpower? Every person on this planet was uniquely created. You were created with gifts and talents and a unique personality, all designed to help you live out your purpose on this earth. But as moms, we have a little something extra because the Lord knew we'd need it.

The Five Mom Superpowers

Let's discover your superpower. As you read through the following five mom superpowers, see which one resonates most. My guess is you may discover multiple ones that fit you. Try to find your favorite, but if you're a mixture, enjoy being that unique mix.

If you want more help figuring out your superpower, visit AlliWorthington.com/momsuperpower or scan this QR code for an easy assessment.

THE CARING MOM

Your superpower is Encouragement.

You are helpful, generous, and nurturing.

The caring mom's superpower is encouragement. You're someone who is always on standby, ready to lift others up. You are helpful, generous, and nurturing. Your kids never have a moment when they feel like you aren't there for them. When your children doubt themselves or feel down in the dumps, you're the person they naturally gravitate toward for a pick-me-up.

Caring moms have perfected the art of lifting others up. You encourage and support. Your belief in your kids' ability to succeed is limitless. You make them feel seen, heard, and supported—a true strength that others recognize and value.

Your Bible verse is 1 Thessalonians 5:11 (NIV).

Therefore encourage one another and build each other up, just as in fact you are doing.

THE RIDE-OR-DIE MOM

Your superpower is Loyalty.

You are trustworthy, strong, and steady.

The ride-or-die mom's superpower is loyalty. You are trustworthy and faithful to your people. You provide a steady, safe, and wonderful home life. Your kids know they can trust you with anything—you will be on their side, no matter what, with quiet resolve. You have a rare unwavering spirit in this turbulent world.

Ride-or-dies are highly dependable and trustworthy. You'd sooner undergo a Brazilian bikini wax than betray your kids' trust. Your children know they can confide in you without reserve. You make them feel valuable, loved, and seen without judgment—a true strength in today's culture.

Your Bible verse is Proverbs 18:24.

> A man of many companions may come to ruin,
>   but there is a friend who sticks closer than a brother.

THE PROTECTOR MOM

Your superpower is Commitment.

You are a mama bear.

The protector mom's superpower is commitment. You're passionate and vocal, someone who loves a challenge and won't back down from it. You are your child's biggest advocate. You stand up for your kids and fight for what's right—for them and everyone around you.

As with any mama bear, there's no hill you won't climb, no mountain you won't move if you think that's what needs to happen for your children. Your example of leadership and strength is a gift to your kids, and they are stronger for it.

Protector moms are highly principled, and you'll dig in your heels and use all your resources for a cause you believe in. Your kids know they are safe with you, as you're their protector. You make them feel strong and capable.

Your Bible verse is Philippians 2:4.

> Let each of you look not only to his own interests, but also to the interests of others.

THE IDEALIST MOM

Your superpower is Excellence.

You are principled, responsible, and trustworthy.

The idealist mom's superpower is excellence. You are highly principled, responsible, and trustworthy. You are known as someone who never veers from what she believes is right. You carry an air of strength that spills over into the environments around you. All that matters is that you follow your moral compass and teach your kids to do the same.

Idealist moms speak the truth and help their children know how to discern right from wrong. Your kids know they can come to you for honesty and structure. You tell it like it is: good, bad, and ugly. You quiet the chaos of their hearts and minds with your steadfast spirit. Those are true strengths in this world of craziness.

Your Bible verse is Proverbs 3:5–6.

> Trust in the LORD with all your heart,
>   and do not lean on your own understanding.
> In all your ways acknowledge him,
>   and he will make straight your paths.

THE CHEERLEADER MOM

Your superpower is Joy.

You are future-focused, energetic, and positive.

The cheerleader mom's superpower is joy. You're future-focused, energetic, and positive, someone who can turn even the most mundane tasks into a joy-filled and exciting experience. When something feels a little stale and boring, it takes mere seconds for you to turn it into a game that engages your kiddos and brightens their spirits. And when your child encounters a rough patch, you are great at helping them refocus and see the silver lining without minimizing their pain.

Cheerleader moms have the uncanny ability to find fun in the most unlikely places. Your skills in navigating life's complications and finding pockets of happiness are unparalleled. You help your children move through the pain to access joy, an ability that will serve them well for life.

Your Bible verse is Psalm 16:11.

> You make known to me the path of life;
>> in your presence there is fullness of joy;
>> at your right hand are pleasures forevermore.

Embrace Your Superpower

It's human nature to focus on things we think we aren't great at—our "weaknesses"—and try to get better at them. But what if we instead focused on our strengths—our mom superpowers?

Keeping your mom superpower in mind helps you to zoom out and remember your own million magic moments.

I told a friend about my bedtime routine with my sons. When they were preschool and elementary ages, I spent ten minutes with each boy at bedtime, just he and I, one-on-one. With the littles, I would read a story or sing a song. With the older boys, we would talk about their day and watch funny videos. And with all the boys, they would list three things they were grateful for, and we would pray together.

My friend Jordan wanted to try my bedtime routine with her girls. She knew how much I loved it and thought it would be a great bonding experience for her and her twin daughters. Fast-forward a couple of weeks. When I asked how the new bedtime routine was going, she told me she hated it. I laughed and asked her why. She told me, "I am not a bedtime mom. By the end of the day, I am done. I want to tuck them in, say a prayer, turn off the light, and dare them to even think about coming out of their rooms. But you know what else I realized? I'm a great morning mom. I love hanging out with my kids in the morning. I make breakfast, we sit at the table, and I read them a story while they eat. It's amazing. I was so focused on trying to be something I'm not instead of just appreciating my strengths!"

Knowing your superpower helps you honor your unique personality. When you lean into who God created you to be, your emotional health improves. That's a real secret of great moms.

For weeks Jordan had focused on trying to be a bedtime mom. She was so focused on doing something she admired about another mom (of course, it's not terrible to try new things) that she felt guilty for not being great at it. The more she focused on (and failed at) the bedtime routine, the guiltier she felt and the more frustrated she became. But embracing her own strengths helped her incorporate good ideas in a way that honored how she's wired. Once her mindset shifted, the experience shifted for everyone.

Her story resonates with me because wishing I had someone else's gift always gets me in trouble. When my kids were little, I hated not being able to do certain things for them because we couldn't afford them. I wanted to be the mom who planned big parties, entertained, and had enough energy to take my kids and their friends on big adventures. But we didn't have the budget for those things, and I felt like I could barely keep my head above water every day. So I focused on what I could do, and that was bedtime. Doing that one thing well helped me embrace the mom I was instead of focusing on the mom I wished I could be.

We didn't take big vacations. I never threw big parties. I did what I could, given what I had at the time. As I learned to embrace my strengths (just like you are doing right now), my emotional health improved. I began to set the atmosphere in our house to be happy, calm, and safe. That helped to take my focus off what I couldn't do and helped my children thrive.

Now my kids celebrate the story of us and the happy childhood they had. **I guess all the ways I thought I was failing my kids weren't important after all.** I bet it's like that for you too. You beat yourself up for things your kids have no idea weren't perfect at the time.

God gave us each our own strengths and gifts. Imagine if we pressed into those things and honored the way God created us. This is what I want to help you do. You and I are going to dive into a new way of thinking about motherhood and ourselves. As a result, you will develop a healthier mindset as we go.

God has a beautiful plan for our children. It's a plan we can't stop, even if we mess up in the day-to-day. That is a life-changing truth. It allows us to move forward in grace as we love our children and ourselves with the unconditional love of God.

As we learn to give ourselves grace, we can step confidently into a new season of motherhood. We are already great moms. Now it's time to drop what's held us back and discover a new way together.

I Want You to Remember

When we zoom in on what we wish were different, or moments we aren't proud of, then of course all we see is the bad. We have to learn to zoom out and look at the big picture of the beautiful, messy, never-ever-perfect life and family God has given us.

According to attachment science, moms of infants have to get it right only 50 percent of the time to be great moms.

If no one has told you lately that you are doing a great job, I'm sorry. You deserve to hear it often. Most of what you do is underappreciated and underacknowledged. Cut yourself some slack, mama. You have permission to give yourself grace. God's grace is sufficient for you and me.

God has a beautiful plan for our children. It's a plan we cannot thwart, even if we mess up in the day-to-day.

Journal and Discussion

♥ When you zoom out, away from the day-to-day feelings of failure, what mothering wins do you see? What shining moments of magic have happened?

♥ How did you feel when you read that we have to get things right only 50 percent of the time?

♥ Ask one of your kids what they love most about you. Did their answer surprise you? Why or why not?

♥ Now ask them what they remember as "magical moments." Did they name the same ones as you? What surprised you about their answers?

PART 2

The Good-Mom Myths

You've seen how modern motherhood is broken. You've discovered your special mom superpower. You know there is a better way to mother without losing yourself and living under the weight of mom guilt. Now it's time to address how we got here in the first place.

A myth is a story that is shared over and over, over time, to explain a belief that is popular but false. Most myths are based in some kernel of truth, which is what makes them so easy to believe. We say to ourselves, "Well, that *sounds* like it could be true." And it is that tiny little nugget of truth that pulls us into its web.

In part 2 we're going to look at the "good-mom myths" that have been passed down through generations of moms, chipping away at our happiness. These good-mom myths are so pervasive in our culture that they feel like truth. As we debunk these myths, we will develop simple new tools that will help us unlock an easier, healthier, and happier way to live.

CHAPTER 4

Myth 1: Good Moms Put Their Families First

Hey there, mama. I know you don't look in Joey's folder, but I need you to actually open his yellow folder tonight and read the papers I sent home."

Ouch. What a gut punch. There is nothing like a public shaming in front of a bunch of other preschool moms to trigger instant mom guilt. Ms. Nancy's voice was dripping with honey, but I received her message loud and clear. Unlike the other "good moms" in the class, I was failing. I couldn't do even the most basic of tasks, like opening the daily folder.

The room spun, and my cheeks were a thousand degrees. I knew then and there I was the most irresponsible, terrible mom in the whole class.

"Oh, of course. Thanks, Ms. Nancy. I'll be sure to take a look. It's been a weird and busy season at home, which I know is no excuse, but I'll do better, I promise. Thanks for letting me know." I blurted out my wordy apology with a forced smile, as much for the other moms listening as for Ms. Nancy.

Grabbing Joey's hand, I scurried out of that classroom, my tail between my legs.

I drove home in tears, thinking about what was making me be such a bad mom. It must be that the time I had put into building my business was hurting my children. If I couldn't even manage to look in a folder every night, what else was I missing?

Was this a sign I should give up my dream of running a business from my living room? I mean, it was a ridiculous dream, right? I didn't have any additional help, and I was building a company while surrounded by kids all the time. How many times had my toddler walked up to me and pushed my computer closed, giggling and saying, "No work, Mommy. No work!"

I told myself I was being selfish and hurting everyone. I should quit.

But no matter how much I wanted to quit, at the end of the day, I couldn't. My husband and I were just getting back on our feet from financial ruin the year before. When the recession of 2008 hit, Mark lost his job and couldn't find another one. We lost our savings, our home, and almost everything we owned.

Until then I'd been a stay-at-home mom who loved being a stay-at-home mom. But as we tried to get back on our feet, I knew it was time for a new season. I needed to work, but I also wanted to be available for our five sons, one of whom was a newborn.

When we lost our house, we stayed with my relatives for the summer while Mark looked for a new job. And I started an online business with a laptop missing a few letters on the keyboard and forty-two dollars of start-up capital. Fast-forward a few months, and my business was growing. I felt proud of myself and my ability to help our family.

I knew in my soul that God led me to build my business. I knew I needed to build it because we needed to dig out of our hole. But I also loved it. I loved learning, trying new things, and not having to get anyone's permission to do work I loved! All throughout history, women have had to get permission to get an education, to get certain jobs, or to be approved by the powers that be to build businesses. Thanks to the power of the internet, I had the world at my fingertips, and with God and Google, I never looked back.

Building my business, learning new skills, and even staying up late at night and working during every naptime were energizing. And while I found motherhood to be the greatest happiness of my life, my work was a fun challenge that I needed in my life. I developed skills and parts of myself I didn't know were in there all along, just waiting to be developed.

But after the folder incident, I felt I was wrong about this being a new season. As a mom of five, I knew seasons of motherhood changed, but my mom guilt told me I was way off base. If building a business was what I was supposed to be doing, I wouldn't be failing my kids, right?

I would have quit that day if we hadn't gone through the bankruptcy and didn't need both our incomes. I would have done what many women do. I would have told myself that my wants were selfish. My needs were hurting my children. And I would have boxed them up and put them on the shelf for someday when the time was right. (But we all know the time is never quite right, is it?) I would have believed the myth that good moms always put their families first and sacrifice their own wants for the greater good. **Thank God I didn't have the financial privilege to quit.**

Ms. Nancy's indictment left me feeling confused, concerned, and condemned. I didn't know what to think. When Mark got home later that night, I unloaded. The anger I felt at being called out, intermingled with the incredible guilt and shame I felt, came spilling out in a jumble of words and tears.

Mark came back with this gem: "Listen, Alli, that preschool

teacher doesn't get to shame you about your priorities. What's so important in a preschool folder? Joey is happy, well-behaved, and doing great. It's not like he's beating up kids in the bathroom. And I doubt she's sending home nuclear codes for you to keep safe. Honestly, do you ever look in the folder?"

I giggled at that picture in my mind and answered with a grin, "On the weekends I look at the folder. So far, no nuclear codes or bathroom fight club warnings."

He finished by reminding me that I get to decide what's important to my family and how I spend my time. The teacher doesn't have the right to shame me for my priorities.

Maybe that's a message for you too?

Good Moms Have Different Priorities

My friend Christy told me that when her boys were little, she wanted to be a stay-at-home mom so badly. Most of her friends from church were stay-at-home moms, and she felt pressured by and even a little envious of the moms who didn't work outside the home.

Eventually, she quit her job (a job she loved). She convinced herself that stay-at-home moms had it made. They didn't have to wake up in a mad rush. They had all day to think about dinner. Their homes were always clean, and because they had more time to devote to their kids, the kids were better behaved.

She laughed when she said, "Alli, I thought that for, like, two weeks. And then I realized I had no idea what the life of a stay-at-home mom looked like. It was incredibly hard. I also realized that being a stay-at-home mom wasn't the life for me. I'm not wired that way. I enjoyed getting up and going to work every day. I enjoyed the time away from my kids. And honestly, I was a better mom after returning to work because I was leaning into my passions and my priorities. Work is a priority. That doesn't mean raising my kids isn't also a priority. The two are related. I realized I felt ashamed that work was a priority for me, and I believed that somehow made me a bad mom."

What mom hasn't been shamed for what she prioritizes?

In my case, I didn't read the school folder every day, but I gave each of my boys ten minutes every single night at bedtime. That was my priority.

Maybe you too have been shamed for what you prioritize.

Have you ever felt mom guilt because of the following?

- You got a store-bought cake for your child's birthday.
- You didn't volunteer to be the snack mom or to participate in the neighborhood carpool.
- You feed your child food that isn't locally sourced organic.
- You didn't breastfeed for three years.
- You feed your kids microwaved meals.
- You let your kids watch TV so you can catch your breath and not lose your mind.

The sheer number of things moms get shamed for is ridiculous. And the majority of what we are shamed for is because others have a different set of priorities. Different isn't wrong. It's just different. **Good moms can have different priorities and still be good moms.** It's that simple.

There are a limited number of hours every day. The number of hours in a day doesn't magically increase with each child you have, though we all wish it worked that way. We can set priorities that work for us and our family because most decisions we make involve a time commitment. Whether it's a decision to breastfeed or bottle feed, buy store-bought baby food or make our own, sign our kids up for a sport or let them play kickball in the backyard with friends.

We make the most of our twenty-four-hour days, we prioritize, we organize, and we continually look for more moments in the day to make sure we are "doing it enough" and spending enough time with our kids.

The crazy part of all this is that studies show that today's moms and dads spend way more time actively engaged with their kids than previous generations did.[1] We have doubled the time we spend engaged with our kids—feeding, talking to, bathing, helping with homework, driving them around—compared with parents fifty years ago.

We spend more and more time mothering while feeling more and more guilty for not being perfect all the time, for having our own dreams, or for not being in three places at once. No wonder it sometimes seems like the time we spend mothering will never be enough.

It Doesn't Have to Be This Way

There is a myth that says the more I give to myself, the less there is for my children. Not only is this untrue, but it's also unhealthy. The only way we overcome this myth is to call it what it is—a lie—and replace it with the truth.

First, making our children our top priority isn't biblical. Christians are called to put God first. **As much as we love our kids, they aren't God.** God commanded us in Deuteronomy 6:5 to prioritize him: "Love the LORD your God with all your heart and with all your soul and with all your strength" (NIV). It's easy to overlook this command, but for Christian parents, it indicates that our kids are not to be our top priority.

Second, caring for ourselves is important. I'm not talking about taking a long shower or going potty without an audience. That's not self-care (though it does feel like a miracle when it

happens). It's nice when our kids give us privacy or the time for a long shower, but it's not enough. I'm talking about having a hobby, enjoying time with friends, dating our spouse, getting a massage—self-care looks different for every one of us. Self-care is about you taking care of you. It's about how you care for your whole self in an ongoing way. Good self-care is necessary for soul care.

My friend Melissa, a professional counselor, taught me that we sometimes struggle to prioritize self-care because we feel like self-care is selfish. But Romans 13:9 tells us to love others as we love ourselves, and Paul tells us in 1 Corinthians 13 that love is patient, love is kind, love keeps no record of wrongs. You will love others best when you learn to love yourself well. You can't give what you don't have.

Think about that for a minute. If we love ourselves, we won't keep a record of our failures. We'll forgive ourselves

> You will love others best when you learn to love yourself well. You can't give what you don't have.

and move on. We'll be patient with ourselves. We'll be kind to ourselves. And when we love ourselves well, caring for our mental, physical, spiritual, and emotional needs, we model that for our kids.

Another way we can love ourselves well is by setting healthy boundaries. Many women don't feel comfortable saying no; most women (especially moms) just say yes, yes, and yes, and we are burned out because of it.

Setting boundaries at home could look like saying, "I'm saying no right now because I need to have some workout time," or "I'm saying no right now because Dad and I need to go on a date night and have some time together." As we set boundaries, we model a love for ourselves that says, "I'm a person of worth and value. God made me just like God made you, and therefore *I'm worth taking care of.*"

Modeling love and boundaries to our kids in a genuine and honest way sets them up to have healthier self-esteem. It's good and holy work to set your children up to prioritize self-care and to have strong boundaries for life.

The Mindset Shift

When we put our needs, wants, and dreams on the shelf, continually sacrificing ourselves at the altar of motherhood, we risk feeling like victims. We ignore God's leading in our lives and may grow bitter as we allow others to set our priorities.

I don't know a single mom who wouldn't say their family is their biggest priority. According to recent research, mothers consistently put taking care of their health last.[2] In managing their health, women spent their time on (ranked in order of time spent): children, pets, older relatives, then their spouse or significant other, and then themselves. Seriously, we spend more time on our dogs' health than our own.

Without proper care, we risk our physical, spiritual, and mental health. What if the most loving thing we could do for our kids was to take care of ourselves?

Imagine if today we all decided to agree on self-care that, for the benefit of both ourselves and our families, we can't skip. What if we all agreed that some things are nonnegotiable for mothers? Melissa was kind enough to give us her

What if the most loving thing we could do for our kids was to take care of ourselves?

nonnegotiables—things all moms need to stay healthy. The good news is that these six ingredients of a happier life are simple, free, and can be added into an already full life.

Six Things Moms Need for Mental Health

1. Sleep

Sleep seven to nine hours. With a newborn, no one gets a glorious eight hours of sleep; it's torture for a few months, and then baby starts to sleep for longer stretches. As kids get older and they go to bed more readily, it's tempting to want to throw a party in celebration and stay up until midnight to revel in your alone time.

But you know what happens next—someone will be up at 5:00 a.m., and you'll be left feeling exhausted, frazzled, and quick-tempered because your brain can't function on so little sleep. To be happier and healthier, you need seven to nine hours.

Don't come at me saying you are fine with four or five hours. Science disagrees. Without enough sleep, our mental health suffers,[3] our immunity is weakened, stress hormones build up and can trigger anxiety and weight gain,[4] and a lack of sleep can even cause early aging and wrinkles.[5] Sleep is a mom's secret weapon to look and feel great.

2. Water

Drink six big glasses of water daily. Dehydration not only puts our internal organs at risk but can also increase our risk of anxiety and depression.[6] Staying hydrated helps our bodies function correctly. It also increases our energy, improves our skin, and helps us concentrate.[7] If you think drinking water is gross, try some flavor (I love coconut LaCroix), or switch to my favorite—decaf green tea.

3. Movement

Move your body. The research is clear: exercise not only boosts your physical health but also helps protect your mental and emotional health. Exercise can ease symptoms of anxiety and depression.[8] One of my sons was going through a particularly rough patch and turned to a daily workout to help him through. He referred to his exercise as "the sadness killer." Movement should be something you enjoy: a walk outside, a Peloton ride, chasing your kids around the block on bikes, a yoga class—whatever makes you happy. You get to decide what works for you. Just get your booty moving for twenty minutes a day.

4. Quiet

Have a daily quiet time for at least five minutes. Read a devotional, pray, worship, practice gratitude, sit quietly—whatever works for you. Science has uncovered what many of us instinctively knew: prayer benefits our mental health. A study showed that those who pray have less depression, enjoy life more, and have higher self-esteem than people who don't pray.[9]

5. Friends

We need friendships with other women. If our main relationships are only with the people in our home, we miss out on the rich texture that friends add to our lives. Our favorite friends help us cope with stress, encourage us, love us, and make us happy. Connect with a friend daily—a call, a text thread, a coffee date. Make time to love your friends and let them love you.

Water

Sleep

Movement

SIX THINGS MOMS NEED FOR MENTAL HEALTH

Quiet

Friends

Breathwork

6. Breathwork

The practice of setting aside a few minutes to do simple deep breathing exercises is surprisingly powerful. Studies show that breathwork reduces stress, boosts the immune system, and helps increase self-awareness.[10] You can download a guide to breathwork from the bonus gifts page at the end of this book.

Prayer, combined with breathwork, has a big impact on our mental and physical health. Taking a few deep breaths helps to reregulate your system and gets you out of the stressful fight-or-flight mode. Often, when we're not taking care of ourselves, we're not connected to our bodies or our emotions until we are overwhelmed by them. Taking a few deep breaths quickly calms everything down.

Often in my adult life I haven't had the energy to take my self-care seriously. But my dedication to giving my kids a happy childhood gave me the kick in the pants I needed to take care of myself. The truth is that an emotionally healthy mom provides her kids with the best environment for thriving; therefore, self-care is never selfish.

Self-care is one of the most loving things a mom can do for herself and her family.

Your Kids Love You More Than You Know

In the sisterhood of motherhood, we are so similar. We beat ourselves up over the smallest things—the yellow folders left unopened, the skipped bath times, the thrown-together meals of fries and chicken nuggets, the missed parent-teacher conferences. And we let our mom guilt steal our joy. The guiltier we feel, the more likely we are to put ourselves last. We forget that putting ourselves last is the worst thing we can do for our families.

No matter what you are beating yourself up for today, I promise that your kids think you hung the moon. In their eyes, you're the best thing since cartoons and Goldfish crackers.

A friend told me recently that she'd been feeling guilty that she'd been spending a lot of time caring for her aged parents and couldn't give much time to her adopted thirteen-year-old twin daughters. To spend some time together, they were watching an episode of *This Is Us*. In the episode, the main character, an African American child adopted by white parents, is attending a group therapy session. In the session, another group member says, "Sometimes I wish a family of another race had never adopted me. I just think it would have been easier."[11]

One of my friend's daughters (who are also of a different race, just like the show's characters) immediately turned to her and said, "Mom, we don't feel that way at all. You are the best mom in the world and the greatest mom for us."

My friend had spent the last several months thinking she was the worst mom ever, but in that moment her daughter erased those negative thoughts in one sentence. She realized that her daughter measured love in a different way than she did. Her daughter measured her love for her as a whole. She measured her mom's love based on security and comfort and the million little things she gets right.

As a mom, you may have ridiculously high expectations of yourself. But your kids already love you more than you know. Being the best you is one of the best things you can do for your family. When you are happy and healthy and whole, they have the best chance at a happy and healthy life.

I Want You to Remember

Good moms can have different priorities and still be good moms.

Studies show that today's moms and dads spend way more time actively engaged with their kids than previous generations. We spend more and more time mothering while feeling more and more guilty for not being perfect all the time, for having our own dreams, or for not being in three places at once.

We are called to love ourselves. If we love ourselves, we won't keep a record of our failures. We'll forgive ourselves and move on. We'll be patient with ourselves. We'll be kind to ourselves. And when we love ourselves well, caring for our own mental, emotional, physical, and spiritual needs, we model that for our kids.

What if the most loving thing we could do for our kids was to take care of ourselves? Because an emotionally healthy mom provides her kids with the best environment for thriving; therefore, self-care is never selfish.

The six things moms need for mental health are sleep, water, movement, quiet, friends, and breathwork.

Journal and Discussion

♥ How have you felt shamed because of what you prioritize?

♥ What have you done to sideline yourself as you mother your babies? Be honest here. No judgment.

♥ What boundaries can you set at home to set an example of caring for yourself as a valuable child of God?

♥ Of the six things moms need for mental health, which one will you put into practice this week?

CHAPTER 5

Myth 2: Good Moms' Kids Are Obedient and Well-Behaved

I was sure my two oldest would become serial killers. This wasn't some random assumption on my part. I had scientific evidence to prove that somewhere between all the snuggles, singing in the car, and vacation Bible school, things had gone terribly awry in our household. Did you know that many serial killers started as animal torturers?[1] Well, it's true, and apparently that's who I was raising.

We were living in a small house in Rhode Island in an idyllic little neighborhood on the water. The street was full of families. Our neighbors were great, and I felt especially safe because our backyard backed up to a police officer's backyard. No trouble was coming to my street!

The baby was down for a nap, and I kicked the big boys outside to play in the yard. I needed five minutes of peace and quiet. As I closed the microwave door, heating my coffee for what was possibly the fourth time that day, something outside caught my eye.

I noticed my five-year-old and three-year-old scurrying back to our yard from the general direction of the neighbor's tiny koi pond. It wasn't that the behavior was suspicious in and of itself, but my maternal Spidey-sense was activated. I couldn't put my finger on it, but I knew something was wrong.

I opened the back door and yelled, "Justin and Jack, what are you boys doing?"

"Nothing, Mom," they yelled in unison. That was the first sign that they were definitely up to something.

When it comes to kids, *nothing is ever nothing*. It's always something, so I called them both onto the porch and tried again, one boy at a time.

"Justin, what are you boys up to?" I questioned, hand on hip.

Again he replied, "Nothing, Mom. We aren't doing nothing."

Justin, my oldest, was an adventurous, energetic, talkative little guy who was always, and I repeat, always, up to something. His younger brother Jack, age three, adored Justin and followed him everywhere.

I looked over at Jack and asked, "Jack, what are you and Justin doing?" Justin gave Jack a death stare and a brotherly jab in the side with his elbow. I smothered a giggle as Jack answered, "Mommy, we aren't doing nuffin," then looked at Justin for approval.

Clearly, my five minutes of peace and quiet weren't going to happen. And given the sketchy circumstances, I decided it was best if they came in where I could keep an eye on them.

Later that afternoon, while Justin was watching TV, I began a methodical interrogation of Jack. I had to find out what they'd been up to. I knew that with the promise of some chocolate milk and Goldfish, I could pry it out of the preschooler.

Both boys were obsessed with a series of documentaries from the BBC featuring cavemen and prehistoric beasts. They

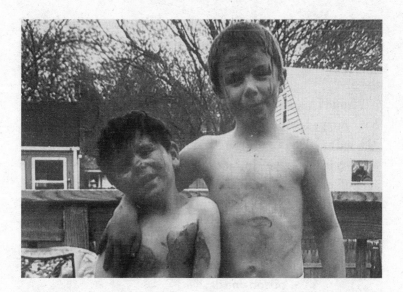

imagined battling woolly mammoths and roasting food over a fire. One July, they refused to wear anything but underwear because it was their version of a loincloth. They used fingerpaint to decorate themselves all over like cavemen. I even bought them pink butterfly nets from the dollar store to help them carry out their caveman hunting adventures.

Under the influence of chocolate and crackers, Jack spilled the beans. Apparently, Justin instigated the whole thing. He reasoned if they wanted to be real cavemen, they had to catch and grill a fish. Of course, somewhere in the back of his mind, he knew this might get them in trouble, so he sent his little brother into the neighbor's pond, hoping to escape blame, should it come to that. At his big brother's prodding, Jack caught a koi fish out of the pond. I imagined his joy at catching a big, beautiful koi out of that little knee-high pond, his pink net teeming with life. What a moment. He was living his caveman dream.

The preschool set isn't really known for being criminal masterminds, nor are they adept hunters and gatherers. Jack uncemoniously dumped the fish onto the gravel at the edge of the koi pond. To their horror, the fish started flopping around in a crazed life-or-death struggle, nothing like they'd seen on the BBC.

Amid squeals that were part horror and part delight, both boys jumped out of the way of the fish's fight for life. Justin devised a plan in a panic; he commanded his little brother to bury the fish in the gravel. In Jack's three-year-old mind, the fish was safe, all covered up and waiting for them to visit again.

I listened in horror to my three-year-old's retelling of the murder.

Later I cried to Mark, "They are animal abusers. Do you know what this means? They'll be in prison one day!"

"Prison?" Mark raised an eyebrow. "I doubt it. They love animals. Plus, you guys go to the zoo all the time. And Justin's hero is the Crocodile Hunter. I don't think we need to worry about prison at this point."

I was undeterred. I genuinely believed I had failed as a mother. The list of how I had failed them was long. I let them be in the backyard without watching them closely enough while the baby napped. I let them run wild covered in fingerpaint and underwear like cavemen all summer. They were on a crime spree, including grand theft koi and first-degree murder of a fish.

I'd ruined them. This was all my fault.

I called my neighbor, the police officer, and explained what had happened. We offered to buy more koi and asked her to scare Justin a little (I knew Jack, at three, had no clue).

In our most serious parental voices, Mark and I told the boys we were going to visit the neighbor and they had to tell her what they had done. Justin was visibly shaken and shuffled across the yard as if going to his execution. In his innocent glory, Jack copied his big brother's serious face but wasn't quite sure what was going on.

Our neighbor came out in her full police uniform. Justin tearfully admitted what they had done and begged for mercy. I asked her if they had to go to jail, and she played along as if she had been thinking for a long time. She cleared her throat and said, "Boys, I know you love animals very much and would never hurt one again. And because you were honest and will replace my fish, I'll give you a second chance."

Justin promised to turn away from his life of crime, and Jack promised never to go near the pond again without a grown-up.

Still, I couldn't shake my sense of failure.

As a young mom of three boys under five, I believed my kids were blank slates. I would input good things—food, education, fun experiences, a lot of snuggles, rules—and the output would be perfect kids (or at least not kids on the way to prison). I could blame toddler tantrums and other little-kid chaos on needing a nap. But as the boys grew, I couldn't blame bad behavior on not enough rest.

I thought I would train up my child in the way he should go and when he was older, he would not depart from it, as the Bible says.[2] I knew I had not intentionally trained my children to steal, kill, and destroy defenseless fish, so clearly my "training up" was way off base.

If they were bad kids, I was a bad mom. I could draw no other conclusion.

Shocking News—It's Not about You

Later that week, I told my neighbor across the street the story and sighed when I told her that I didn't know where I went wrong with the boys. She laughed at me. With beautiful silver hair, a broad smile, and wisdom that comes from raising a slew of kids, she admonished, "You didn't do anything wrong. Not everything kids do is a reflection of their moms. Kids will be kids," she said, adding with a soft chuckle, *"and not everything your kids do is about you."*

"How is it not about me?" I asked with a slight hysterical rise in my voice.

She said, "Do you seriously believe that everything your kids do wrong is because you are a bad mom? Think about it! Do you think that every time someone makes a bad decision, it's because God is a bad father?"

I stared at her, speechless. She'd made her point. I assumed I was a bad mom because I was raising fish killers. I had fallen for the myth that good moms' kids are obedient and well-behaved. This myth is one of the most damaging because every single day, our kids make decisions that fly in the face of the training we have given them. Sometimes kids just misbehave.

Here's a great example—I know I have trained my boys to look both ways before crossing a street. I know this because I started when they were babies in strollers. I'd stop at the edge of the street and say to my infant son, "Always look both ways before you cross the street. Look to the right, then the left, then back to the right, and *then* if it's clear, you can cross."

Then I'd roll their little stroller across the street. As they got older, I continued this lesson anytime we crossed a street. The lesson was the same every time. "Look to the right, to the left, to the right again, *then* cross if it is clear."

But you know what? I can't even tell you how many times those boys have thrown my careful training right out the window and run into the street chasing a ball, a brother, a skateboard, or a squirrel. Sometimes kids just do what they want.

The same is true of teens. My friend Janie told me anytime

she was with her kids and saw teens acting crazy in public, she commented about how poorly behaved they were. She would tell her boys, "I know when you're old enough to go out on your own, you'll make better decisions." Then one night, she got a phone call from a security guard at the mall because her teens were climbing up the rails of the down escalator and making videos of TikTok dances with their friends.

The truth is toddlers, ten-year-olds, and teens sometimes make their own decisions based on their personalities and their environment, no matter how many times we've told them what's appropriate or not.

What's crazy is I held on to the myth that my boys' behavior was about me until I had more kids and they got a bit older. As I watched each of them develop and grow into their own little person, I realized that although their training was the same, their behaviors were different.

Each of my boys is completely different from the others. They all look different, act different, and have different personalities, senses of humor, and temperaments. They were all raised pretty much the same but are so different.

Some of my boys are quiet and introverted, some are loud and extroverted, some love sports, some are gamers, and some want to be left alone to read a great book. They are each unique, and Mark and I did not *make them* that way. God gave them their personalities, their loves, their dislikes, their tempers (or lack thereof), and their zest for adventure. I am not God, and living with my sons reminds me of that fact every day. Have enough children and you'll have at least one wild child whom you pray stays out of jail—it keeps you humble.

As kids grow, we hopefully make peace with all the ways they will make mistakes (so many ways—who knew there were that many ways to get in trouble?). The best we can do is to teach kids their boundaries, how to make wise decisions, how to repair relationships, how to make amends when they mess up, and how to take responsibility for and bounce back from failure.

We have the challenging but wonderful job of helping their maturity unfold.

When God says in Proverbs 22:6 to "train up a child in the way he should go; even when he is old he will not depart from it," I believe he is telling you to help your children embrace the way he made them. In doing so, you can guide them to discover and understand the unique aspects of who they are and how they are made. We do this by helping our kids identify their talents, gifts, and strengths. As our children mature in the understanding of who they are, and who God is, they will begin to understand who God created them to be. With that solid footing, they will not soon stray to a different path.

It was never a promise that how you raise your kids will guarantee who they become as adults. Of course I wish it were that way. But that was never part of God's plan.

Proverbs 22:6 doesn't say your kids will be perfect, thus magically making you a perfect mom. It says that you, as a mother, play a significant role in guiding your children to become who they were created to be.

A mother's job is to love, guide, and disciple. The result of her work is between the child and God.

There is no such thing as a perfect mother. And if perfection were possible, it would completely mess up the kids. Seriously, suppose a mother did everything perfectly. What would happen when the kids left the house and discovered a world of imperfect people? What would happen when a cruel friend hurt their feelings, their boss didn't give them grace in a situation, or their spouse lost their temper? I'll tell you what would happen. **The person raised by a perfect mom would melt down** because they wouldn't have the mental toughness and emotional intelligence to deal with imperfect people. They never would have had the chance to develop those skills before they left home.

Good moms make mistakes every day, and the best moms apologize and repair relationships when needed. This gives their kids the best education about experiencing failure, seeking restoration, resolving conflict, and moving forward.

This is great news. Let's welcome imperfection because our imperfection is exactly what our kids need.

The Game Changer—Differentiation

My friend Phoebe is a mom and a counselor. She taught me how smart, loving, intentional mothers can fall into the trap of believing that good moms' kids are always well-behaved.

We know we aren't God. We know we aren't all-powerful, but something in us holds on to the lie that if our kids misbehave, it's because we are bad moms. We sometimes hold on to that lie because we are overly connected to our kids.

During pregnancy, we—mother and child—are one person made up of two people. Then the baby is born, and we are two different people, separate and whole. In that early stage we are often connected through physical contact in some way. We mothers

Differentiation allows us to say:

"I'm responsible for myself and any response to this situation."

constantly carry our babies around, feeding them, rocking them, soothing them.

Over time, mother and child slowly differentiate in each other's minds. The mom sees herself again as an individual. As the years go on, the child sees themselves as unique and separate from the mother.

Differentiation is good and healthy. It allows for boundaries and emotional health. Differentiation says I am me and you are you. We are different people. And this concept is the foundation of healthy boundaries. We are individual people, and we are responsible for ourselves—our health, mindset, and behaviors. When our kids are babies, of course, we are responsible for them. But as our kids get older, we both acknowledge and respect them as individuals.

Phoebe shared that *a lack of differentiation could be why we believe the myth that our kids' behavior is our fault.* Failure to differentiate can result in emotional enmeshment. Enmeshment means we are "overly connected to another person's needs so badly, we lose touch with our own needs, goals, desires, and feelings."[3]

Do you know how myths become truth in our minds? Myths are based on a kernel of truth, and that little nugget of truth makes it easy for us to believe the lie. So is it true that our kids' bad behavior is our fault?

It is true that how we parent *does* affect our kids. We have influence over our kids, and our influence can shape how our kids behave. But our influence can't *control* how our kids behave. Do you see the difference?

Influence with our children is a gift God has given us. We can't guarantee any outcome because we live in a world where free will exists and bad things happen. But we can give our kids powerful gifts. We can share our values, our faith, our love for fried chicken, and our disdain for running unless being chased. As we

IS THIS MY FAULT?

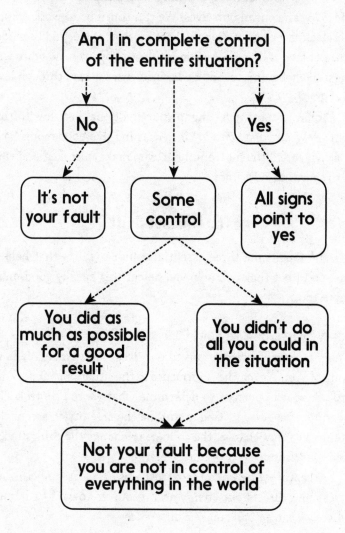

share those things, we influence our children. If they grow up and become marathon runners, we can't be blamed for that; we tried. They have free will, and we are not to control them.

But we can control something very powerful in our child's life. We can control ourselves. We can continue to work on our mindset, to be as emotionally healthy as possible, and to model a life of love and grace. A child influenced by love and grace will most likely become an adult who influences others through love and grace.

Today, you are investing in your emotional health with this journey we are on together. We're learning that good moms have kids who are different from them, who make mistakes, and who also share in God's grace.

The Mindset Shift

Phoebe taught me three essential mindset shifts that helped me, and I bet they will help you defeat this sneaky good-mom myth too.

1. Ask Yourself, "What Can I Control Here?"

There are very few situations in our lives that we actually have control over. We may have influence in the situation, but not control. So it is important to determine what we *can* control. The Serenity Prayer says, "God, grant me the serenity to accept the things I cannot change, the courage to change the things I can, and the wisdom to know the difference."

Accepting what we can't control helps us release unnecessary stress and directs our energy and resources toward situations where we can actually make a difference.

A great way to assess what we can control is to place the situation into one of three categories:

1. What do I have no control over?
2. What do I have influence over?
3. What do I have control over?

But how do we decide what category the situation belongs in?

First, you have to understand what agency is. **Agency is being able to make choices and take action on our own.** If we have agency in the process *and* the outcome, we have control. This means we can both decide and act independently.

If we have agency in the process *but not* the outcome, we have influence.

If we have no agency in the process *or* the outcome, we have no control or influence.

WHAT CAN I CONTROL?

1 What do I have no control over?   **2** What do I have influence over?   **3** What do I have control over?

Here is a quick and easy example. The weather report says a tornado is coming my way. (If you are a mom of toddlers or teens, feel free to replace the word *tornado* accordingly!) What do I do?

I have no control over the weather.

I also can't control my family's response to the tornado warning. But I can *influence* how my family reacts to a tornado warning. I can influence where in our house we will go for safety. I can influence the environment, deciding whether it will be one of chaos and confusion or calm and confidence. I have agency in the process of getting everything down to the basement but not in the outcome—I can't control whether they stay calm or have a wild Nerf gun battle down the steps.

However, I *can* control how *I* respond to the tornado warning.

I have both the ability to decide how I will respond and the ability to act. I have agency in both the process and the outcome.

Where I have control, I thank God for giving me the strength, courage, and wisdom to exercise control. Where I have influence, I thank God for giving me the strength, courage, and wisdom to use the influence he has given me. And where I have no control, I ask God for the strength, courage, and wisdom to allow him to work as only he can, since he *does* have agency in all things.

2. Reflect on All the Things You Got Right

Another powerful tool to shift your mindset is to build the habit of reflecting daily on what you did right. Then, in your mind, rehearse your successes instead of your mistakes.

A day spent mentally beating yourself up is miserable. A day spent giving yourself grace for your mistakes and focusing on good things you did is better for you and your kids. Instead of staying focused on what went wrong, train your brain to think about what went right.

This difference won't just make your days easier, but also will model emotional health for your kids.

The mistake-focused mom lives knee-deep in the quicksand of shame and regret. Meanwhile, the growth-focused mom is continually covered in grace. She finds hope each day when she asks, "What did I get right today?"

I'd rather be a mom covered in grace than consumed by guilt.

3. Take the Long View

The daily battles, heartaches, and frustrations of parenting can wear us down like stones under running water. The suffering of the day, whether it's a kid who has a tantrum at the store, breaks curfew, or is mean to a friend on the playground, can be overwhelming.

I'D RATHER BE A MOM COVERED IN GRACE THAN CONSUMED BY GUILT.

But if we look at life with a long-term view, we can see it in a new way. Yes, the crisis of the day may be an issue, but it's also important to **look at your child's trajectory**. Sure, she may be hell on wheels some days, but how is your four-year-old doing really?

Is she more patient than when she was three?

Is she better at sharing than she was six months ago?

Is she showing more empathy and care for those around her than she did three months ago?

When you take the long view and look at the trajectory of her life, she's probably going to be just fine.

Maturity happens slowly. All we need to do is be an influence for the better and help that trajectory stay strong in the right direction.

FOCUS ON YOUR CHILD'S TRAJECTORY

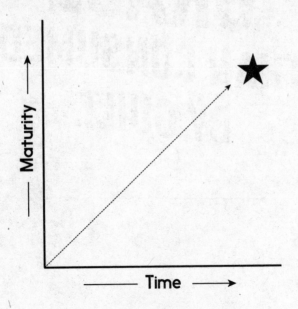

We know that the days go by slowly but the years fly by. Some days, we pray we'll just get through the day. But one day we look up and realize that all those hard days, mixed with all the great days, added up to years of raising some pretty terrific children.

You're doing a great job, mom.

Oh, and I promised Justin and Jack I would tell you that they never went to jail. They love animals, but they will *obliterate* any spider that dares invade our home.

I Want You to Remember

The person raised by a perfect mom would melt down because they wouldn't have the mental toughness and emotional intelligence to deal with imperfect people.

Good moms make mistakes every day, and the best moms apologize and repair relationships when needed. This gives her kids the best education about experiencing failure, seeking restoration, resolving conflict, and moving forward.

Differentiation is the healthy process of mother and child seeing themselves as separate people. It allows for boundaries and emotional health. Failure to differentiate can result in emotional enmeshment. Enmeshment means we are overly connected to another person's needs so badly, we lose touch with our own needs, goals, desires, and feelings.

We can control something very powerful in our child's life. We can control ourselves. We can continue to work on our mindset, to be as emotionally healthy as possible, and to model a life of love and grace. A child influenced by love and grace will most likely become an adult who influences others through love and grace.

A great way to assess what we can control is to sort situations into one of three categories:

1. What do I have no control over?
2. What do I have influence over?
3. What do I have control over?

The mistake-focused mom lives knee-deep in the quicksand of shame and regret. Meanwhile, the growth-focused mom is continually covered in grace. She finds hope each day when she asks, "What did I get right today?"

Journal and Discussion

♥ As you think back over the mothering you've done so far, what is one thing you beat yourself up about that you need to let go of?

♥ Where are you taking responsibility for your child in unhealthy and unwarranted ways?

♥ What does differentiation need to look like for you?

♥ What comes to mind when you think about what you can control, what you have influence over, and what you can't control concerning your children?

♥ What's something you've gotten right as a mom that you're really proud of?

CHAPTER 6

Myth 3: Good Moms Don't Get Angry

Do you have a friend who seems perfect? She never yells and seems calm no matter what? For me, that's Ashley. She always looks lovely, her kids are always well-behaved, and she never has fries and toys fall out of her minivan when she opens the door.

I used to think Ashley was the most perfect mom ever, and I wasn't sure we could even be friends, and then she told me the most hilarious story about losing her temper.

Ashley's husband was out of town on a business trip. She and her two sons, ages four and five, were returning home from church one Wednesday night. It was pouring rain and the power was out, so she couldn't open the garage door. The front door was locked, and she didn't have her keys to the house since she'd planned on entering through the garage. Then she remembered all the times her husband had lectured her about forgetting to lock the back door, and she prayed, "God, let me have left that door unlocked tonight."

She turned to her five-year-old in the back seat and said, "Hey buddy, I'm going to need you to do me a brave, big boy favor and climb the fence and see if the back door is unlocked."

Immediately her little guy panicked and started wailing, insisting that he wasn't brave, that he was afraid of the dark and the rain, and that he couldn't climb the fence.

She told me, "The more he cried, the madder I got. I was mad at my husband for being gone. I was mad at myself for forgetting my keys. I was even mad at the thunderstorm. I was mad at everything. And I just lost it. I mean, I *lost* it. I got out of my car in the pouring rain, opened the back door, and yelled in his face, 'Just climb the damn fence and open the back door!'"

His poor little lip quivered. He was so shocked that she had raised her voice. *She* was shocked she had cussed at him. He pitifully nodded, opened his car door, and ran to the place at their fence where he'd learned to climb over. Within minutes he was at the front door, soaking wet, sobbing, and saying, "I did it, Mama. I was brave. Please don't be mad, and don't say no more bad words."

Ashley reacted that night in the rain after years of stuffing down her frustration. She sighed as she told me, "My husband had traveled for years. And every time there was a problem, I'd solved it on my own. But I was worn out. I had zero tools for dealing with my anger. I felt trapped, and I guess I snapped. And now I'll forever be known for the damn fence meltdown."

Pressure, Pressure, Pressure

Ashley's story hits home, doesn't it?

The pressure of day-to-day frustrations builds and builds and builds. It's because of a never-ending stream of a million little things. It's temper tantrums, sick kids, runaway dogs, broken toys, and lost lovies. It's burned dinners, missed meetings, school projects, and last-minute teacher conferences. As moms, we aren't supposed to get frustrated, because good moms don't get angry, right? We just stuff it down, over and over again, until inevitably we snap over the mundane—over lost keys or traveling husbands or spilled milk.

Not only have we believed the myth that good moms don't get angry, but many of us have been taught that anger, in general, is an unhealthy or "bad" emotion. We've adopted the "mad is bad" mindset for many reasons.

You may have grown up in a home where anger was never expressed, only repressed. And it led you to believe that getting angry must be a bad thing, something to be avoided at all costs. Or perhaps you grew up in a home that was violent and chaotic. It led you to fear that all anger would result in verbal or physical abuse; therefore, anger equaled pain. Or maybe you grew up in a home sheltered from signs of anger. Arguments between your parents happened in private, leading you to assume your parents didn't get angry. Therefore, if you ever felt angry, you felt confused, scared, and isolated.

A few lucky ones grew up in homes where their parents handled anger in a healthy way, but these families tend to be the exception, not the rule.

As we dive into the truth about anger, let's uncover the myth that good moms don't get angry. Once we know the truth, we can develop a healthier mindset together.

Expert guidance is crucial when we are learning about anger. I've spent months interviewing friends who are brilliant therapists, and I'm excited to share all I have learned.

The Mindset Shift

The good news is, anger is a normal, healthy, natural emotion that God gave us intentionally. The two primary reasons God gave us anger are for our protection and for responding to injustice. Most of us are familiar with anger and injustice. Seeing people being abused and mistreated triggers what we call righteous anger.

Anger is also the emotion that protects us when we feel threatened. It triggers our fight-or-flight response. When we are vulnerable and the most at risk, our anger is there to protect us. That's why our anger is a quick defense when we are tired, hungry, in pain, injured, afraid, and so on.[1]

Though anger is natural, we also live in an imperfect world. Our anger can convince us we are justified even when we aren't. That's why God tells us, "'In your anger do not sin': Do not let the sun go down while you are still angry, and do not give the devil a foothold."[2] He recognizes that we will be angry. But he reminds us not to sin in our anger.

The truth is that good moms do get angry.

Of course, we sometimes respond to our anger in unhealthy ways. But feeling angry is not bad in and of itself. **It is rarely our anger that is the problem, but more often our response to it.**

Sometimes you feel angry because the baby hasn't slept through the night in weeks, and you yell at your spouse about the shoes in the middle of the floor. You aren't actually mad about the shoes. You are mad that you are sleep deprived, and your nerves are as fried as the chicken tenders you left in the oven too long. Yelling about the shoes is the unhealthy response to your anger.

Sometimes you feel angry because you have a little kid who flips out and loses their mind because a drop of water is on the outside of their sippy cup. Or heaven forbid that their sock feels funny on their pinkie toe. You aren't actually mad that they are acting like a typical toddler. You are mad because this type of behavior is genuinely annoying when it comes at you constantly, and before long you feel out of control.

Sometimes you feel angry because your husband is blind to

the laundry basket and your bedroom looks like a yard sale of clothing thrown all over. You aren't actually angry because your husband doesn't care about the laundry; you are hurt because you feel he doesn't care about what you want.

Sometimes you feel angry because opinionated Aunt Ellen won't stop commenting on how you are raising your kids. You aren't actually angry about her opinions; you are angry because her comments make you doubt your parenting skills.

And sometimes you feel angry at yourself for not being the mom you thought you would be. That anger is centered on a lie you have believed about yourself. A lie that says you are inadequate, incapable, and imperfect. A lie that says, "You are not enough."

Processing Our Anger

Anger is an emotion that requires a bit of self-reflection to understand. It's not just, "I'm mad," and that's it. There's always more to it. As my friend Renee, a licensed clinical social worker, taught me, **emotions are information that tell us something**. And our anger is information that tells us something is wrong.

Once we calm down a bit after our anger flares, we can do the needed self-reflection to understand what was really happening when we got angry.

Here are some self-reflection questions I ask myself after I have felt angry:

What was going on around me?
What were my unmet expectations?
How did I feel?
What was my automatic thought or the story I told myself?
How did my anger get resolved?

SELF-REFLECTION QUESTIONS:

What was going on around me?

  What were my
unmet expectations?

How did I feel?

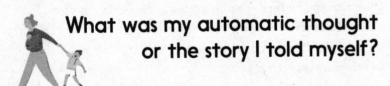 What was my automatic thought
or the story I told myself?

How did my anger
get resolved?

I asked Ashley these questions about her fence story.

What was going on around you (what were the environmental factors)?
> *It was dark, raining, and I was locked out of the house.*

Environmental factors can explain why our anger flared up. They don't explain the root of the anger itself, but they can help us understand why we responded in an unhealthy way. Bad weather and unexpected circumstances are just a couple of environmental factors.

I know having other people witness my kid's bad behavior can be an environmental factor. Nothing brings on a shame storm like a public viewing of a toddler's meltdown in the checkout line.

What were your unmet expectations?
> *I expected the garage door to open; it was really that simple. That was the catalyst.*

Sometimes it is simple. We expect things to be a certain way, but they aren't. Other times, unmet expectations are more complex. The root of Ashley's angry outburst wasn't the garage door, the forgotten keys, or the rainstorm. Her pressure had been building for weeks, maybe even months.

Her broader unmet expectation was that her husband would be there, a partner in their parenting journey. But instead, he was often absent from the life she had envisioned for them.

How did you feel?
> *I felt frustrated. I was afraid, stuck outside with my kids, in the dark, alone. And I felt stupid for forgetting my house keys.*

Emotions are just our bodies' way of reacting to things happening around us. They're not good or bad on their own. But how we feel about those emotions is different. How we feel about our emotions is based on our past experiences and what we believe might happen in the future. Ashley was angry with herself. (Emotion.) She felt incompetent for forgetting her keys. She based her feelings on past negative experiences connected to forgetting things. (She forgot her credit card at the restaurant. She forgot to take snacks when she was the snack mom. And she forgot her most recent dentist appointment, to name a few.)

What was your automatic thought or the story you told yourself?

Ashley's automatic thought was, "Ashley, this is all your fault. If you were more organized, this wouldn't have happened." That story transitioned to, "This is all his fault. If he didn't travel all the time, I wouldn't be faced with these issues alone."

Again, this question helps us understand our feelings. Understanding our feelings helps us understand our anger. Ashley's first story was based on the past and her belief that she was disorganized. Her second story was based on both the present and the future. She felt alone and also felt as if her husband's constant travel might never change.

How did the anger get resolved?
I got the door open, but I felt sad that I had yelled and cussed at my child. I had to take some time to calm myself, and then I apologized to my child for losing my temper.

Using these questions can help us process our anger. Even so, sometimes we calm down and sort through our anger but forget to go back to the person we hurt. Don't forget to close the loop. Closing the loop means returning to the person we included in our angry outburst and asking for forgiveness. That allows for healthy closure and a way to move forward.

Walking Back through the Story

Our anger is often rooted in some physiological need to protect ourselves, and it takes some effort to dig in and understand what we are angry about.

Most of the time, we can't even say what we need because our focus is on the needs of others. And it's been so long since we thought about our own needs that we are completely out of touch with them.

What else is our anger telling us? Do we need coffee, a date night, a nap, time with friends, or five seconds of peace and quiet? Or is there something else we need?

My friend Alexandria shared with me a strategy she learned in therapy. The strategy, called walking back, allows us to walk back through the story of our emotions after we get angry, often uncovering a need that has not been met. She shared this example with me from her own marriage.

Moms have been focused on the needs of others so long that we don't know what we need.

I was angry because my husband couldn't hear me. He had a childhood illness that had left him with hearing loss. I wasn't really angry that he couldn't hear me, I was angry that he wouldn't wear his hearing aids at home. He only wore them

> at work, on the phone with clients, at conferences, etc. And because it was such a sore spot for me, anytime we got into an argument, I brought up (passionately) that he refused to wear his hearing aids.

At first, she thought she was angry because his refusal to wear his hearing aids hurt her feelings. But she walked back a little further, asking herself *why* it hurt her feelings.

> After I thought for a minute, I realized something much deeper. We have a busy home—the baby, the toddler, and a very barky beagle. And then his sister moved in with us. If we ever needed to have a private conversation, we had to go into another room because I knew he wouldn't be able to hear a whisper. And even if we went into another room, I still had to talk loudly so he could hear me. This kept me from talking to him in general because I knew he wouldn't be able to hear me, but everyone else would. So I kept things I needed to talk about bottled up inside. My real frustration wasn't that he couldn't hear. It was that I didn't feel important enough for him to listen to me. And that makes me feel isolated, lonely, and depressed.

Once Alexandria walked back through the story, she understood why she was so angry about her husband not wearing his hearing aids, and she could tell him how it affected her. Then she helped him understand she wanted to feel like she was important to him so she would feel less lonely in their marriage.

Understanding your emotions allows you to identify your unmet needs, which often cause anger. Having grace for yourself and staying curious about your emotions in a nonjudgmental way allow you to develop a healthy way to manage anger.

How to Handle Anger in a Healthy Way

MAD ISN'T BAD

All right, friend, we've established that anger isn't something to feel shame about. Good moms can and do get angry. Mad isn't bad. Now let's tackle what to do with our anger when it pops up.

1. Practice Self-Regulation

When my kids were all young, there were years I felt some degree of anger for a good part of my waking hours. The number of times we get pushed, triggered, and harassed in a day should give us credit for Navy SEAL training. Moms are the best of the best when it comes to our level of restraint in harrowing situations.

After the birth of my second son, I had postpartum depression and took a low-dose antidepressant. Years later, my doctor and I decided it was time to wean myself off the medication. Sure enough, I didn't seem to be depressed anymore, but I noticed I got mad and yelled a lot more.

I am a big fan of better living through modern chemistry; I survived my postpartum phase (quite literally) because of it. After stopping the medication, I realized it was time to develop some good habits for handling my anger in a healthy way. I couldn't just go around yelling at my kids all day.

I developed a coping mechanism for when my anger would flare. It calmed me and made the kids slow down and pay attention. I would slowly, out loud, count to ten.

1...2...3...4...5...6...7...8...9...10

Two things happened when I started counting and breathing deeply on each count. The kids realized I was mad and stood down from whatever nonsense they were doing. This allowed me to calm down enough not to freak out and yell at them. Of course, this only worked well with kids after the age of five or so. Kids are adorable but irrational before that point.

My therapist friends told me that this is an example of self-regulation. Self-regulation is your ability to manage your thoughts, emotions, and actions. I was managing my emotions by calming myself down. We self-regulate when we pause between a trigger or feeling and our actions. **The pause between the trigger and how we respond to that trigger is where the magic happens.**

Pausing gives us time to think before we act. It also allows our children to see and learn the tool for themselves. They realize we are not victims of our emotions, and we don't have to act out in a way that is unhealthy.

SELF-REGULATION STOPS SELF-DESTRUCTION

Self-regulation allows us to act in a way we won't regret. We can get angry without lashing out. As Ephesians 4:26 puts it, we can be angry without sinning. We can feel sad without eating the whole Haagen-Dazs. We can feel lonely without texting that unhealthy friend.

Your ability to self-regulate your emotions and take that pause between trigger and response can provide the foundation your children will build on to self-regulate as well.

2. Be Proactive and Reduce Triggers

My friend Renee taught me the importance of being proactive when it comes to our emotions, especially anger. Again, self-reflection helps us understand our triggers *after* we get angry. We can use that self-reflection to help create an environment with fewer triggers. This practice allows us to explore what makes us angry, which allows us to connect the dots and find patterns. **Once we see patterns in our anger and identify the triggers, we can be proactive and create an environment that is less triggering.**

For example, Mary, an advertising executive in Seattle, got what she described as her dream job. Best of all, it had free onsite daycare for her twin fourteen-month-olds. Even though it was a forty-five-minute commute from her house, she told herself it was worth it. But after a few weeks of commuting, it seemed her dream job was creating a nightmare for her afternoons and evenings.

Halfway home, the twins would start crying because they were hungry. Some days, rush-hour traffic was worse than others, thanks to bad weather or bad accidents. Mary yelled at other drivers on the road. And she yelled at the girls to stay awake in the back seat. If they fell asleep on the way home, they wouldn't go to bed on time, and *Lord knows* Mary needed those girls to go to bed on time. By the time she arrived home most nights, her nerves were fried.

One day, when Mary was on a postcommute tirade, her husband said, "We can't go on like this. I want you to have this job. I know you love it. You've worked hard to get it. But you can't be angry the rest of your life."

Mary realized the biggest trigger to her anger was getting home late and the girls getting off schedule. And the biggest factor in what time they arrived home was the traffic, something she had zero control over.

One way to create an environment with fewer triggers was to change what time they got home. So she asked her boss if she could come in an hour early and leave an hour early, allowing her to miss rush-hour traffic. It worked like a charm. When Mary removed the trigger, her anger was gone because she could meet her own needs and get home before her children were hangry.

Sometimes a solution can be simple. We might feel stuck, which can trigger our anger. But getting creative, even in small ways, can help us proactively address our triggers.

Proactively addressing your triggers is a brilliant way to minimize stress and angry outbursts.

- Tired of picking up the kids' dolls out of your beautiful bathtub? Bathe the kids in their bathroom.
- Losing your mind because your kids won't sort the toys into the right buckets? Give them fewer buckets and adopt the mindset "Put away is still okay!"
- Hangry kids getting off the bus and ruining your afternoon chill? Pack a snack in their lunchbox to eat on the way home.
- Sick and tired of unruly teenagers stealing your phone charger? Hide it in your panty drawer; they won't look in there!

Of course, to proactively address your triggers, you have to know what they are. At the end of this chapter, you'll have a chance to take a minute to jot down what you've gotten angry about in the last few weeks. Then do a little self-reflection and identify the triggers. Exploring what makes us angry and proactively addressing what we can is a game changer for managing our anger.

3. Talk to Someone

Find safe friends who don't pretend they are perfect. Talk about this stuff with them. It can be hard to find friends we can trust with our most vulnerable stories. But we have to find friends who are also doing the hard work of self-reflection and self-regulation and are brave enough to share their stories with us too.

Once you find those safe friends who also tell you about their real lives, you'll discover we all live similar lives behind closed doors. No matter how perfect we may look on social media, no one's kids are that cute and well-behaved. Your toddler is not the only one who headbutted you, pulled all the books off the shelf, melted down because you picked the wrong color straw, and pooped in the bathtub *all in one day*. Toddler terrors and teenage tyrants exist in real life. And as awesome as our husbands are, no one's husband is as constantly loving and attentive as social media would have us believe.

Talking to friends is great, but sometimes you need a professional to talk to. I can't say enough about how beneficial therapy has been for me personally and as a parent. It's been one of the best things I have done for my children. As we've learned, our emotional health impacts our children's emotional health more than almost anything else. Because of that, investing in therapy is one of the most loving things we can do for ourselves and our families.

Our anger is a great indicator of our mental health. It helps us understand we may have an unmet need, which is also true about our children's anger. Learning how to express anger in a healthy way is critical to busting the good-mom myth that good moms don't get angry.

Our anger is a great indicator of our mental health.

As we develop some healthy habits to control our anger, we proactively set aside the guilt and shame that come with it. And as we model those healthy habits, our kids learn to do the same, setting them up to have a healthy mindset about their own anger.

Mom life comes at you hard and fast some days. Sleepless nights, days filled with toddlers and tantrums and teenagers, isolation, and crazy schedules—they are enough to make even the most patient mom lose it.

Mad doesn't make you bad. It makes you human, a person with needs and desires that often go unmet as the demands of motherhood take precedence. Cut yourself some slack, give yourself some grace, and if the heavens part and bestow a miracle on you, take a nap.

I Want You to Remember

Anger isn't something to feel shame about. Good moms can and do get angry. Mad isn't bad.

Emotions are data that signal the things we care about. And anger is information that tells us something is wrong.

Here are some self-reflection questions to ask yourself after you have felt angry:

- What was going on around me?
- What were my unmet expectations?
- How did I feel?
- What was my automatic thought or the story I told myself?
- How did my anger get resolved?

Walking back through the story of our emotions often uncovers a need that has not been met.

Self-regulation allows us to act in a way we won't regret. We self-regulate when we pause between a trigger or feeling and our actions. The pause between the trigger and how we respond to that trigger is where the magic happens.

Proactively addressing your triggers is a brilliant way to minimize stress and angry outbursts.

Journal and Discussion

♥ Anger is a true and valid emotion, but sometimes it's masking something else. If you were to excavate your anger, what would you find underneath? Frustration? Loneliness? Exhaustion? Something else? Why do you think this thing shows up as anger?

♥ What are some of your anger triggers? Take a minute to jot down what you've gotten angry about in the last few weeks. Then do a little self-reflection and identify the triggers. Exploring what makes us angry and proactively addressing what we can is a game changer for managing our anger.

♥ Brainstorm a practice you can use to self-regulate when feeling triggered. It could be counting, praying, taking a walk, etc.

CHAPTER 7

Myth 4: Good Moms Protect Their Children from Pain

I had stopped praying other than to occasionally tell God how mad I was at him. I was still a believer, worshiped on Sunday mornings, trusted my soul to heaven, and knew God loved me, but I had no desire to talk to him.

That was when I knew I needed to get my butt into therapy. I didn't know what was going on inside me, but I knew it had created a deep anger with God.

I was a few months into the darkest season of my life. Two of my sons were suffering (and are still suffering to some degree) from chronic daily migraines. The illness came on years apart for the boys. Jack's migraines started in high school, and we assumed it was from a football-related concussion. And then our youngest son, Jeremiah, developed them out of the blue in early puberty.

I'm not one to sit around and do nothing. We've been to every specialist, neurologist, chiropractor, and pain specialist who would let me in the door. We tested our home for mold and poor air quality. We tried allergy shots. We've done extreme diet plans from prestigious universities. We've tried every medicine the FDA has approved for each age group. Our older son has tried Botox, nerve injections, acupuncture, and devices with electric currents promising to reduce pain. You name it—we've tried it.

After spending tens of thousands of dollars and countless hours with doctors who all guarantee they can cure constant migraines, still no cure.

But none of those disappointments compared to my disappointment that God had not healed my sons. God, the maker of heaven and earth, the eternal creator of my sons, would not relieve their pain. Over the years, I spent hours praying and begging him to remove the pain. I thanked him in advance that he would heal them. I had many people praying for them, and it became painful when they would ask for updates because I had only bad news to share.

Surely somewhere among great doctors and the Great Physician, there was an answer to my sons' pain. Over and over again, I placed my hope in both medicine and miracles, only to have them crushed beneath the waves of one disappointment after another.

Year after year, month after month, day after day, and nothing happened. *Nothing happened.* The pain intensified in them and in me.

If you have suffered the cycle of dashed hopes, whether from the aftermath of a traumatic event, illness, chronic pain, infertility, or another experience that has had you begging for the hand of God, then you know where I was mentally, physically, and spiritually.

In the fall of 2020, both boys took a nosedive. My then twelve-year-old, Jeremiah, was in so much pain he stayed in his room twenty-two to twenty-three hours a day with the lights off.

I brought every meal up to him and could not speak above a whisper because even the sound of my voice was excruciating.

He spent *three months* like this. His neurologist gave him a new medication that failed and another that *might* help within ninety days. My hope for Christmas was that Jeremiah would feel well enough to be with the rest of the family and open his gifts with us.

With each passing day, my disappointment turned to anger. I was mad at the illness, mad at the world, and mad at God. My grief was so powerful I feared that if I let myself feel it, my heart would be like a black hole, sucking everything up, including me.

My heart was shipwrecked on a dark island, and the storm never stopped slamming me against the jagged rocks. My pain broke me into a million pieces, ripped at every seam. Everything was wrong, nothing worked, and I was losing hope that I could experience a life that felt good again. It felt safer to stay angry than to let myself grieve. My anger would protect me, whereas my grief might consume me.

I was able to compartmentalize during the day when I was working. I kept coaching my clients, recording podcasts, and creating curriculum for students in my programs, all while keeping up appearances for my husband and our other boys—doing all the mom things while being attentive and loving. I delivered meals to their bedrooms, talking to one son in pain, while whispering to the other in his dark room. I didn't cry; I didn't feel. I didn't want to feel. I was numb.

My therapist, Amy, helped me find myself again and process my pain over time. I learned to open and heal my heart despite the grief and connect with God again.

If you've ever had a small child angry with you, you know your heart still explodes at how much you love them, even in the midst of a terrible-twos tantrum. When your moody teenager gives you the silent treatment, you would still walk over hot coals to protect them, even though they say the most obnoxious things. And above all else, you know their anger will pass, even when they lose it in a rage.

This was God and me. I stayed mad at him for over a year. I told him how mad I was, often. He didn't get angry with me for not being able to process my pain. He didn't quit loving me or judge me when I lost myself and my desire to talk to him. He didn't condemn me for the grief that I let come between us. God waited patiently for me, with love and understanding.

The months rolled by, and both boys found treatment plans that gave them some relief. Jeremiah was able to go back to school this year, and we hope Jack will be able to finally start college. The pain isn't gone yet, but we are getting closer. Their smiles returned, dark bedrooms were left empty during the day, and God was there through it all.

God didn't cause my pain, nor did he protect me from it. But he stayed with me through it and led me to people who could help me process it.

When it comes to our children's pain, that's our role too. The good-mom myth that says it's our job to protect our kids from pain is wrong. Pain is inevitable. It's part of life—yours, mine, theirs. Good moms don't protect their kids from all pain. They teach them how to handle it when it comes their way.

The Mindset Shift

In 1994 the American Academy of Pediatrics recommended mothers begin torturing their babies with a practice lovingly called "tummy time." It came in response to the Back to Sleep campaign, launched to reduce the number of SIDS-related deaths.

Unfortunately, back-sleeping took away the time babies spent on their tummies in their cribs. This now missing "tummy time" was critical to their motor development. While avoiding one serious infant health crisis, they created a new stress crisis for moms everywhere. Let me explain.

Dr. Karen Adolph, director of the NYU Infant Action Laboratory, said, "The more waking hours babies spend on their tummy, the earlier on average they will roll over, push up in a prone position, and crawl."[1]

Without tummy time, babies would be like the people on the *Axiom* in the movie *WALL-E* who never use their bodies. They look like big blobs and have sat so long they can't walk, so their bodies turned to jelly from lack of use.

No mother wants that. We want our babies to push up, crawl, and walk. Then we want them to run, drive, do all our errands, and then eventually go away to college. And finally, we want them to get married, give us grandchildren, and start tummy time with their own children. It's the circle of life.

But wow, those first few tries at tummy time are traumatic. The baby screams and bangs their little face in exhaustion and anger, and the whole experience leaves both mother and child shaken.

Though painful, tummy time is necessary. Yes, our heart breaks as our little one cries out to be rescued. But we know that rescuing them from this short-term pain would create a long-term problem for them. **In our wisdom, we allow them to experience discomfort, knowing that pain will give them strength to live a great life.**

As moms, we know that tummy time is just the beginning of the pain our kids will experience. With every new experience comes the possibility of pain. If you think about it, childhood is basically a military-grade challenge course.

They have to learn to walk (and fall).

They have to learn to climb (and fall).

They have to learn to ride a bike (and fall).

They have to learn to make friends (and fail), learn new things in school (and fail), and fall in love (and fail).

Try, fail; try, fail; try, fail. It's ongoing for their entire life.

But as they fail, they learn they can get back up and try again. And eventually, given enough opportunities to try and fail, they will succeed.

The secret to your child's success is in your willingness to let them fail and experience the pain that comes with their mistakes.

Of course, I'm not saying we let our kids suffer needlessly. But pain, struggle, and discomfort work together to build strength. Without struggles to overcome, children may develop the core belief that they can't handle hard things and see themselves as fragile or weak. Jumping in and solving every problem teaches kids they can't handle problems. **Keeping kids protected from situations where they could feel pain has the unintended consequence of teaching them that they can't handle disappointment.**

And it doesn't stop with early childhood. If we kneecap our kids by accidentally stopping them from learning how to deal with the pain of life, we've set them up for an adulthood they won't be able to handle.

Dan Jones, a past president of the Association for University and College Counseling Center Directors, shared, "They [college students] haven't developed skills in how to soothe themselves because their parents have solved all their problems and removed the obstacles." He continued, "They don't seem to have as much grit as previous generations."[2]

Without struggles to overcome, it's easy for a child to develop the core belief that they can't handle hard things and to view themselves as fragile or weak.

We don't learn how to ride a bike without the pain of skinned knees, bruised elbows, and a few tears. We don't learn how to deal with conflict without hurting others and getting hurt. We don't build grit without struggle. **We don't learn that we can do hard things, survive pain, and rise above our challenges if we never have any challenges to begin with.**

Our role as mothers is not to allow *excessive* pain. If I could snap my fingers, my boys' pain from their illness would disappear. I would also take away the pain of broken hearts, hurt feelings from overzealous coaches, and every other difficulty. But I can't do that, and other than the pain of illness, nor should I.

Reality and research teach us that we aren't the hero or the villain in our kid's journey with discomfort or pain. Age-appropriate pain, be it having tummy time or failing a test, is necessary for our children's development.

How to Think about Pain

When it comes to our children being in pain, we can't help ourselves. We are wired to rescue them. We are called mama bears for a reason. You mess with our babies, and we will come at you hard and fast. Hell hath no fury like a mama whose baby is hurting. And it doesn't matter if the baby is two or twenty.

But as tempting and innate as it is, rescuing our children from pain is not always the right thing to do. We must learn new ways to think about their pain and our response to it.

1. Identify the Type of Painful Situation

Our kids will go through a million painful experiences in their lives, just like we have. Our role is to identify each situation on its own merit, determining whether we should step in.

Ask yourself these questions:

1. Is my child in physical danger? If yes, step in. If no, stand by.
2. Is my child at risk of abuse or trauma? If yes, step in. If no, stand by.
3. Is this pain helpful? If no, step in. If yes, stand by.

Let's use some examples to run through these questions.

A young child climbing a ladder unsupervised:
> Is my child in physical danger? Yes. Step in. Pain from this injury is not "helpful" pain. It is unhelpful to their physical development.

A child crying out in "pain" from hearing no in the grocery store when she wants candy:
> Is my child in physical danger? No.
> Is my child at risk of abuse or trauma? No.
> Is this pain helpful? Yes. She is learning she can't have everything she wants all the time.

A child struggling in class because of a learning disability:
> Is my child in physical danger? No.
> Is my child at risk of abuse or trauma? Maybe.
> Is this pain helpful? No, it is unhelpful to their academic success and their self-esteem. Allowing a child to fail when they need help is inappropriate.

A child making bad grades because he decided homework is lame:
> This is helpful pain because he is learning the consequences of his behavior.

A child struggling with feeling left out:
> This can be helpful pain because this is something she will experience throughout her lifetime. You get the opportunity to help her navigate that pain.

SHOULD I STEP IN?

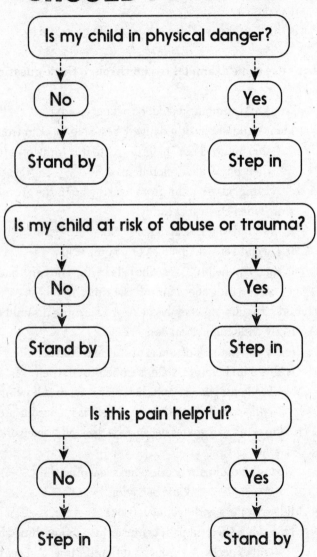

Is my child in physical danger?

No → Stand by

Yes → Step in

Is my child at risk of abuse or trauma?

No → Stand by

Yes → Step in

Is this pain helpful?

No → Step in

Yes → Stand by

But if a child is being bullied and left out, that is not helpful. Step in, mama. Step in quick.

You get the idea. Once you are in the habit of assessing your child's pain, you'll run through these questions in a split second. You will be able to know when to step in and when to stand by.

2. Acknowledge the Pain

Pain is pain, even if it is character-developing pain. Children are damaged when a parent denies or minimizes their pain. When your daughter feels left out because she didn't get invited to a party, acknowledge that it hurts to be left out. Saying something like, "Suck it up, buttercup—you're not going to get invited to everything," might be true. But it might leave your daughter feeling shunned by her peers and shamed by her parents. Acknowledging your child's pain, giving them empathy, and talking about difficult situations are key.

When your little one falls and skins their knee, a simple "Ouch, I bet that hurt" goes much further than an "It's okay." Even as an adult, when I'm in pain and someone says, "It's okay," I want to say, "No, no, it is clearly *not* okay."

When your child struggles with a subject in school, you can say, "I know this is hard. It's frustrating not to understand something right away."

When your daughter doesn't get chosen for the cheerleading squad, or that part in the school play, or first chair in band, acknowledge her hurt. You can say, "I know how hard you worked for this. I'm very sorry you didn't get picked." Acknowledging her effort and her pain will go a long way in raising an emotionally healthy child.

3. Encourage Your Child's Attempts to Deal with Their Challenges

When my boys were little, I took them to a playground near our neighborhood. The oldest, who was nine, took off running for the "big slide," as he called it. His brother, who was seven, followed close behind him, feeling confident about his ability to climb the big ladder. And of course, the baby, a four-year-old of the third-born variety, was hard on their heels.

I sat down on a nearby bench, noticing a mom in hover mode near the bottom of the slide. She was tending to what I correctly guessed was her firstborn preschooler. (I was a hover-mom with my firstborn too.) As my four-year-old put his foot on the bottom rung of the ladder, the other mom called out to me, "Is he okay?" I smiled, nodded, and yelled a reassuring, "Oh, yes, he's done it many times!" Clearly she was questioning my sanity and my skills as a mom.

Of course, he didn't start out climbing by himself. I'd stood at the bottom of that ladder many times, encouraging him as he climbed, just as I'd done with his brothers before him. At first I climbed with him, always just one step below him. Then I stood a few steps down, holding his little bottom as he climbed. Each time he tried, I increased the distance between us until he could climb all the way on his own.

The more you encourage your child to take steps to overcome their struggles, the more they will feel empowered to overcome each new challenge. As your child begins to meet challenges head-on (climbing a slide, riding a bike, dealing with a difficult friend, working with a demanding teacher), your child will build resilience and self-confidence.

A child who builds resilience feels that they can handle the challenges and pain that inevitably happen in life. Children build self-confidence by finding ways to solve the pain and struggles they experience.

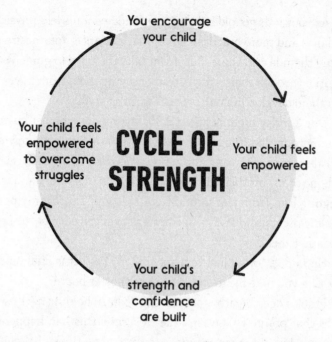

4. Think of Yourself as the Guide

You can't protect your children from all painful situations, nor should you. But you can play the role of a wise guide. You can give them love and show them you believe they can solve their problems. And most importantly, you give them the resources and tools they need to overcome their challenges.

When your kids are little, this is not an easy task. One big wrong move on their part, and you're in the ER with stitches. So the role of guiding them through their pain looks more like trying to keep them in one piece. But as they grow, you have the opportunity and responsibility to guide in a different way.

In the early years, "guiding" your children through their pain is mostly physical training, like with my boys on the slide. Yes, they will fall while riding their bikes, but you'll be there encouraging them to get back up, then stepping back and allowing them to try again.

As your kids get older, being their guide entails less physical guidance and more practical, emotional guidance. Your desire to rescue them is still there. But if you take the time to guide your children through their pain instead of saving them from it, you'll help them develop lifelong problem-solving skills.

One Sunday night at about 8:30, my middle schooler busted into my room like the house was on fire. I was immediately on high alert, ready to spring into action. Was there a fire? A burglar? Had one of his brothers tied up one of the younger ones and was dangling him from the second-floor balcony? I threw my book onto my nightstand and swung my legs over the edge of the bed. It was go time.

He said, "Mom, I just remembered my project is due tomorrow. Can you take me to the store to get poster board?"

I took a deep breath, not realizing I'd been holding my breath up to that point. This wasn't the first time this had happened with this kid. I'd extended grace to him many times. I thought about getting dressed and driving him to the store. But then my rational, nonrescuing mind took over, and I calmly said, "No."

"No?" he questioned. "Are you serious? You're joking, right? Funny one, Mom."

"I'm not joking," I said, sitting back on my bed and picking up the book I'd been reading.

"But if you don't help me, I'll fail," he cautioned.

"Yes. You might. Maybe you can use something besides poster board. I bet you'll figure it out." My voice was reassuring and encouraging. And with that, I swung my feet back into bed, pulled the comforter over my legs, and started reading again.

As he stormed out of my room, I heard a lot of frustrated wailing on his part, but I resisted the urge to get up. The next morning, he came down for breakfast, project in hand. He had taped together multiple pieces of notebook paper to create his own "poster board," and he seemed so happy with his work. He got a B-minus.

I didn't rescue him. I offered some guidance to move his brain from freak-out mode to problem-solving mode, and I let him sink or swim.

Your children will experience many types of pain throughout their childhood, teenage years, and adulthood. Being their guide will look different in every season.

In our family, the situation with my sons' illness has caused pain more extreme than what I hope most families ever go through. I can't solve it, but I will spend my days providing every tool and resource—medically and psychologically—I can to help them cope.

I'm their guide, not their God. I can't take it all away, but I can guide them as they learn to cope and grow through the pain.

5. Manage Your Emotions

I was chatting with my therapist friend Phoebe about the myth that good moms protect their children from pain. She shared that one of the most important things we can do is to examine our own relationship with pain.

With my sons' pain, I had to come to peace with the truth that I didn't cause it and can't fix it. My role is to be there for them and give every resource humanly possible to help them deal with the pain, hopefully lessen it, and eventually overcome it.

We help our kids build healthy self-confidence by giving them love, empathy, and tools so they can manage their struggles. And we have to manage our own anxiety so we don't swoop in and solve every problem.

Research shows that anxious parents raise anxious kids. According to Dr. Alison Escalante, "Anxious overparenting is producing fearful kids who think they can't do anything for themselves. The same behavior we do out of love (trying to take their pain away) can actually cause more pain long term if we aren't courageous enough to do some self-examination of our feelings and emotions that drive our behavior."[3]

On the flip side, emotionally healthy parents have the best chance of raising emotionally healthy children. Examining and dealing with and managing our emotions is a healing gift for ourselves and a strong example for our children.

6. Remember the Healer

Seeing my children in pain is one of my greatest heartaches. Even if I know their pain will somehow be used for good, I struggle with wanting to save them from their pain with every fiber of my being. On the hardest days, I remind myself of this simple truth from Psalm 139:13–16 (paraphrased for moms):

> You created their inmost being;
> > you knit them together in the womb.
> I praise you because they are fearfully and
> > wonderfully made;
> > your works are wonderful;
> > I know that full well.
> Their frame was not hidden from you
> > when they were made in the secret place,
> > when they were woven together in the depths of the earth.
> Your eyes saw their unformed body;
> > all the days ordained for them were written in your book
> > before one of them came to be.

I take great comfort in knowing, trusting, and believing that God knows everything about my children. He numbered the hairs on their heads (Luke 12:7), keeps track of all their sorrows and collects their tears in a bottle (Psalm 56:8), and ordained all their days before even one of them came to be (Psalm 139:16).

He is God, and he chose me to be their mother. I know my role, and I know his. He is not the source of their pain; he is the source of their strength. And I am here to remind them of that truth.

In this world, we will see trouble, we will know pain, and we will have times we feel shipwrecked against the jagged rocks. Unfortunately, our kids will too.

The truth is that good moms don't always protect their kids from pain. Good moms protect them from unnecessary awful things, of course. But we also have learned that some pain, some struggle, and some difficulty are necessary. And helping our children develop the skills to overcome struggles and setbacks is one of the best things we can do for them. This important work helps them build resilience and gives them the gifts of self-confidence, less anxiety, and a healthier mindset.

I Want You to Remember

Good moms don't protect their kids from pain; they teach them how to handle it when it comes their way.

Without struggles to overcome, children may develop the core belief that they can't handle hard things and see themselves as fragile or weak. We don't learn that we can do hard things, survive pain, and rise above our challenges if we never have any challenges to begin with.

Keeping kids protected from situations where they could feel pain has the unintended consequence of teaching them that they can't handle disappointment.

Use these questions to determine whether to step in:

- Is my child in physical danger? If yes, step in. If no, stand by.
- Is my child at risk of abuse or trauma? If yes, step in. If no, stand by.
- Is this pain helpful? If no, step in. If yes, stand by.

The more you encourage your child to take steps to overcome their struggles, the more they will feel empowered to overcome each new challenge. As your child begins to meet challenges head-on, they will build resilience and self-confidence.

Research shows that anxious parents raise anxious kids. Anxious overparenting can create fearful kids who think they can't do anything for themselves. When we try to take away their pain out of love, we can actually cause more pain long term if we don't do some self-examination of our feelings and emotions that drive our behavior.

Journal and Discussion

♥ Have you ever felt anger over a struggle your child had? What has that looked like in your life?

♥ Have you ever thought about how some struggles and pain can benefit and equip your kids?

♥ Having a tool to assess whether you should step in is helpful. Do you have any current situations where the flowchart will help you decide when to step in?

CHAPTER 8

Myth 5: Good Moms Can Do It All

If you invite me to a Halloween party, I'm showing up as Wonder Woman. I'm here for her vibe. She's strong, capable, independent, intelligent, and rocks those gold cuff bracelets like nobody's business. She doesn't have FOMO; she isn't a people pleaser; she's never anxious. She has somehow achieved the elusive work-life balance, and she for sure *woke up like that.*

But can you even imagine how much we would hate Wonder Woman if she were a mom next door? Forget that she can fly and has superstrength. This lady never makes mistakes. She always knows what to do and looks perfect doing it.

Meanwhile, I'm over here with five-day hair, driving to school while trying to remember if I brushed my teeth this morning and obsessing over messing up my younger teens, scarring them for life because I let them watch a movie with bad words last night.

Of course, if your kids were lucky enough to have Wonder Woman as their mom, that *could* be pretty great. Who needs the hassle of a school bus ride or car line when your mom can fly you to school in her invisible plane? They'd have a hot breakfast every day, along with their favorite lunch, including crustless sandwiches painstakingly cut into perfect triangles.

She'd never be late for anything, wouldn't miss an event because of work, and would never raise her voice unless it was to cheer them on. They would never have to know the pain of a mother who hurt their feelings, disappointed them, wasn't available to them 24/7, and didn't have the right answer for every childhood and adolescent problem that came along.

On the other hand, just as we can't relate to Wonder Woman's perfect self, our kids wouldn't either. She would never be able to empathize with them when life felt overwhelming. She's never been overwhelmed. She's never been picked last, looked over, rejected, failed, heartbroken, shamed because she wasn't good enough, or any other day-to-day struggle your kids have. She would not be able to relate to them as you can.

Sure, Wonder Woman is an amazing superhero. Would we expect anything less from a mythical goddess? But she'd be a terrible mom. Those superpowers and tight abs can only take you so far, you know? There's way more to being a great mom than getting everything right all the time, no matter what the world would have us believe. Perfection is overrated.

A perfect mom would completely mess up her kids.

Imagine growing up with a mom who never makes a mistake—someone who is always right, does everything with ease, and has perfected the art of, well, everything.

First off, you would grow up wondering what was wrong with you. If your mom is perfect, why are you such a flawed human being? As a teen and young adult, in hard times, you would struggle to adjust to a world that wasn't perfect. A world where people were fallible and always made mistakes would be overwhelming.

WONDER WOMAN WOULD BE A TERRIBLE MOM.

We can stop striving for perfection. **We can look at our mistakes from a different perspective. What if every mistake we make helps our children build resilience, tolerance, and empathy?** What if this helps our children see that good people sometimes make awful mistakes? This insight will help them understand real life and build their character as they grow and learn.

We mess up because we are human. When we make mistakes and then do the work to repair the damage they caused (to people, situations, etc.), it is a chance for our kids to watch and learn.

If we never expose our children to our failures or imperfections, they won't know the first thing about dealing with people in the real world. When we make mistakes, we're teaching our kids how to deal with other imperfect people they'll run into throughout their lives.

There is a dangerous idea in "mom culture" right now. It says that if we don't get everything right, we are hurting our kids. This belief says every little thing we do affects their future, as if their lives depend on it. Reality doesn't work that way.

I had five kids under the age of ten, and I was just surviving. I wasn't trying to be perfect, and I didn't give a rip about what all the parenting magazines had to say. We have never lived around family, and in those early years, we for sure didn't have money to pay for help. We raised the boys on *Blue's Clues* and Star Wars marathons, and they had spaghetti or frozen lasagna for dinner at least three times a week.

One time I loaded the kids up for a trip to Target, only to arrive at the store with one shoeless kid because he wasn't "into shoes" anymore. He had secretly ditched them before we left the house. I shrugged my shoulders and went with it. I decided raising "shoeless Joe" was less stressful than him having a meltdown every time I tried to get him to put shoes on.

Seriously, the TV was always on at our house, I've never made

What if every mistake you make helps your children build resilience, tolerance, and empathy?

What if it helps your children understand that good people can make awful mistakes, enriching their character as they grow and learn?

them eat salads, and never once have we done family devotionals more than once a year. Those things are great, and hats off to the moms who do them. They weren't the exact tactics I used with my family. It's not that I didn't care about their brains or their digestive systems or their relationship with God. I care about all those things, but I knew I could raise well-rounded kids while also trusting myself as a mom. I trusted myself to do things in a way I could manage without driving myself crazy in the process. I didn't have to do things like other moms do them.

Three of my boys are now adults—one is annoyingly healthy and sends me his organic meal prep tips, one was valedictorian of his class (TV does not, in fact, rot the brain), and the other has made peace with wearing shoes in public after all.

Your kids don't need perfection. They need a mom who is wonderfully made, flawed, and continually growing and investing in herself.

I started my motherhood journey not striving for perfection but striving to survive. Over time my survival instincts naturally led to having a flexible mindset. After years of being forced to prioritize under pressure, I could more easily recognize what mattered (and what definitely did not). For me, that was growth, and it built an off-ramp from the perfectionist mentality. I went from a negative mindset (survivalism) to a positive one (flexibility).

A mom modeling growth and adaptability gives her children the greatest gift. She's teaching them to develop character in adversity, navigate difficult situations with both boundaries and humility, and have grace for themselves and others.

Surface Pressure

Can we both agree that chasing perfection is a sure way to suck the joy out of motherhood? From the moment we discover we will become a mom, whether through birth, adoption, or marriage, we are bombarded with messages that strike fear in any woman's heart.

The pressure not to fail at motherhood is high. We read books that warn of the sixty billion ways we can mess up our kids. We skim articles that tell us fifty things we need to do to be great mothers. Then the pressure is on. Not only do we have to do it all, but we also have to do it all perfectly.

The movie *Encanto* is an absolute delight and is inescapable for any parent with a child under ten. As with most things in life, if your kids love it, you'd better learn to love it or make peace with living with it. In *Encanto*, we meet Luisa, the oldest sister, who has super-

THREE WAYS YOU ARE MESSING UP YOUR KIDS

Screen Time Makes Kids Grow Tails

Child's Future Ruined by Mom Who Lost Her Temper

Mom and Toddler Banned for Life from Target

strength. She sings a song, "Surface Pressure," that has the power to make most moms stop in their tracks and cry.

She sings about how strong she is with everything she carries, and it is the perfect anthem for the brokenness of modern motherhood. As Luisa sings about her strength, she wonders who she is if she can't handle it all. She dreams of escaping the crushing weight of expectations, of having some time and energy for joy.

I polled thousands of women on Instagram and asked this simple question: "Did the song 'Surface Pressure' resonate with you?" And 87 percent of women answered with "100%. That's my theme song." A whopping 87 percent—that's a bonkers number of yeses! It's clear what we are all experiencing, isn't it?

My friend Kylie told me that *Encanto* was on in the living

room as she cleaned up dinner and listened to the lyrics for the first time. She stared at the screen, motionless, then went and cried in her bedroom because, as she said, "That cartoon song was the perfect metaphor for my life. It's all on me—the emotional toll, the daycare details, the birthday parties, the seven million little things I need to keep up with. Matt [her husband] is a great dad, but he doesn't keep up with it like I do. It's all on me!"

Another friend of mine, Bri, a single mom with two little ones, said that after her divorce, it was all up to her because her ex-husband moved out of state. There was no every-other-weekend visitation with dad to give her time to get things done without littles underfoot. There was no taking turns missing work when one of the kids was sick. There was only her, all the time. From sunup to sundown, the weight of caring for her kids was all on her shoulders. And the pressure was crushing her.

I began reading women's feelings about the song all over the internet. Those feelings are perfectly summed up by writer and comedian Sarah Aswell:

> We women and mothers are socialized to be like Louisa [sic], from the time we're girls and helping our siblings and around the house, and then once we become moms and partners. We're taught that helping our family and hiding our feelings is the best combination—at least for others. We're taught that we can have superhuman strength—as long as we put aside our own needs and wants. We're told to ignore the pressure and be grateful for what we have—even if it's breaking us down. We're told to put our accomplishments before ourselves.
>
> How can we not tear up when we hear her sing *that she is pretty sure she is worthless if she is not of service?* In light of the labor—physically, mentally, and emotionally—we've given over the years, the lyrics hit home.

And how great it is that our kids are watching this movie and learning that being the strongest in the family doesn't mean you should shoulder everyone's burdens?[1]

The surface pressure we feel as moms takes our need to do it all and combines it with our need to do it perfectly. (Heaven forbid we should make a mistake, let anyone down, let something slip through the cracks, or take a break.) It creates in us a perfect storm of anxiety-ridden thought patterns.

"Surface Pressure" resonates because it reveals the under-the-surface secret we moms have been carrying for generations. It's a secret that asks, "Who am I if I can't carry it all?"

The Shouldstorm

It's not your fault you feel this way. We all feel it to some degree because the pressure to be a perfect parent is so pervasive in our culture that it seems like gospel truth. It's as if *everything* we do matters and we'll ruin our kids if we make any mistakes. It's not as if anyone ever sat us down and told us this explicitly, but the message is so ingrained in society that it feels like a foundational truth.

As pediatrician Dr. Alison Escalante said, "The moment we become parents, we are inducted into a culture that pushes perfectionistic parenting. We are told everything we do matters and warned of all the harm that will come to our children if we mess up. The culture of parenting criticism tells us that we are fully responsible for our kids and everything that happens to them."[2]

Dr. Escalante saw a continual stream of moms who had ever-increasing anxiety about their children's health and well-being. The moms seemed unable to tell the difference between what was important and what wasn't. They listened to their friends, their social media circles, and their neighbor's cousin's mother-in-law who was a school nurse twenty years ago. This information overload created what Escalante calls a "shouldstorm." A shouldstorm happens when moms tell themselves they should be doing a million things. I'm sure you've been caught in your own shouldstorm a time or two.

The shouldstorm creates a set of impossible rules that tell us:

1. We need to get it right. All the time.
2. We are fully responsible for our children emotionally, physically, academically, and spiritually.
3. The worst thing that could happen to our kids is an uncomfortable emotion, because we somehow confuse emotions with trauma.[3]

No wonder modern motherhood is crushing us.

She explained that the culture of anxiety over every little thing that is infecting moms is infecting the kids too. Worried moms raise worried kids. In fact, one in three children will meet the criteria for an anxiety disorder by the age of eighteen.[4]

Research shows that anxious parents raise anxious kids. Anxious overparenting produces fearful kids who think they can't do things for themselves. Research also shows that perfectionistic parents who alternate between demanding and overnurturing raise demanding kids who expect to be kept comfortable.

If more is caught than taught, we must invest in our emotional health.

On the other hand, isn't it comforting to know that the opposite can also be true? If anxious overparenting produces fearful kids, then maybe, just maybe, we can free ourselves from the impossible standards that culture has set for us. When we do, our kids have a great shot at being freed from that same anxiety.

The Mother Load

The truth is that no other generation of moms has ever been held to such impossible standards, been so hard on themselves, or been so hyperfocused on every little detail of parenting. The weight of this responsibility is part of our mental load.

Mental load is the cognitive effort involved in managing your work, relationships, a family, and a household.[5] It's the whole enchilada, everything a person manages throughout any given day. Mental load includes our responsibilities and all the daily decisions we make: from getting the kids to school and scheduling work meetings, to walking the dog, calling the doctor, choosing a tutor, and deciding what to cook for dinner. But more importantly, it includes the mental weight of those things.

Everyone has a mental load, but I think for moms it goes a step further. Not only do we carry the weight of our responsibilities but we carry the weight of perfection along with it. I call it the mother load.

MENTAL LOAD + MOTHERHOOD = MOTHER LOAD

Mothers are exhausted from the day-to-day demands of work and family, but also the mother load of keeping it all together at work (at home and outside the home), building our businesses, and growing personally, while also worrying whether we're hampering our children's educational futures and ruining their spiritual development and wondering whether we're measuring up to everyone else's expectations of us as mothers. Oh, and also keeping tabs on the household stock of hand soap and toilet paper, scheduling vet appointments, and buying gifts for nieces, and a million other little things.

The mother load is an invisible and unwelcome enemy, covered in chaos, surrounded by stress, and wrapped in worry. In chapter 10 you'll discover strategies to help you get out from under the weight of the mother load. In chapter 12 you will learn communication techniques to help you hand off some of the mental load to your spouse.

The broken culture of modern motherhood may tell us that it's a mom's job to handle every last detail on her own, or that moms have to worry about every single decision we make. There's a better way, and we can turn this tide together, for ourselves and our children.

Arm Yourself with Facts

The way to heal the damage done to motherhood is to arm yourself with facts. And I mean legitimate facts based on decades of research, not your best friend's opinion or junk facts your great-aunt Susie saw in a meme on social media.

We live in a culture that is trying to make us believe we have to be perfect, and it's making us anxious about mothering. Luckily, we also live in a time when brilliant researchers are pulling together data from decades of study.

Remember when we discovered that we have to get it right only about 50 percent of the time to be amazing moms? Learning that fact was my lightbulb moment. What if I started studying? Could I find well-respected research to answer my mothering questions?

It turns out I could! I have a *Remaining You While Raising Them* bonus gift workbook with tools, discussion guides, a guide to breathwork, and all the research and data for you. You'll find a QR code at the back of this book so you can dive into all the details. But for now, I want to share one big research-backed truth with you: there is much more of a genetic component in how our children turn out than we realize.

We've probably all heard that kids who grow up surrounded by books will do better in school, right? They will achieve more and make better grades. Who hasn't gone out and bought a million books hoping to give their child an advantage? But what if it's not so cut-and-dried? What if those kids who did well in school had homes full of books because the parents were naturally smart? They passed the genes down to their kids. Maybe it wasn't the presence of books or even being read to that gave those kids an advantage; maybe it was genetics.

Achievement in sports is largely genetic as well. Some kids have it; some don't. Having a large family made that clear in my house. Some of our boys are athletic wonders like their dad, and some, like me, could hurt themselves walking room to room. No matter how much we pushed the kids to achieve greatness in some areas, the genes gave natural abilities and unfortunately many limitations.

Genetics play a bigger role than I could have imagined. Studies like the Minnesota Twin Study have looked at twins separated at birth and raised in different homes. The story that blew me away was about identical twins James Arthur Springer and James Edward Lewis. They spent only their first four weeks of life together and then were reunited after thirty-nine years.

I hope you are sitting down for this next part. They each married and divorced a woman named Linda, and their second wives were named Betty. They both named their son the same name. One brother named his son James Allan and the other James Alan. As kids, they each had a dog they named Toy, and they both had law enforcement training and worked as deputy sheriffs. Unbelievable, right? Of course, some similarities could be more coincidence than genetics, but there's more.

The twins had the same type of tension headaches that became migraines. (This resonates with me as our two boys and my stepdaughter have migraines, so they likely have a genetic propensity for migraines as well.)

The study goes on to show that they shared the same hobbies and school class preferences and both vacationed at the same three-block-long beach near St. Petersburg, Florida, and drove Chevrolets.[6]

Even though they were raised in separate homes, they were genetically predisposed to be alike in many ways. They both grew up in healthy homes where their natural traits flourished. If one of them grew up in a home full of severe neglect or abuse, of course, we would likely see that the toxic environment had altered the natural traits.

Our culture conditions us to believe that our child's personality and future are determined *only* by our actions. The truth is, their personality and future result from a mix of our parenting, their environment, and genetics.

A recent study calculated that in the first year of a baby's life, the parents face 1,750 difficult decisions.[7] Breast or bottle? Cosleep or sleep train? Paci or no paci? Silent sleep environments or white noise machines? Those are just a few of the decisions made in the first year of life. Similarly, many of the other decisions parents make may not have much long-term impact either.

Some examples:

- One of the largest randomized controlled trials on breastfeeding found that it had no significant long-term effect on a variety of outcomes.[8]
- A careful study of television use among preschoolers

found that TV had no long-term effects on child test scores.[9]

- A randomized trial suggests that teaching kids cognitively demanding games like chess doesn't make them smarter in the long run.[10]

It's a hard but freeing truth when we realize our kids are not blank slates. The responsibility for who your child will be is not on you alone.

We can wear ourselves out trying to control every little detail of our children's lives. But the truth is that God has encoded them with their own personalities, strengths, weaknesses, and abilities.

I love that God has a plan for each of my children and I can't change who they are supposed to be. He "knit them together" and is creating in them a beautiful masterpiece of who they will become. No matter what we call it—DNA, genetic coding, God-ordained—it's all the same: a predetermined picture of their life story.

Now, I'm not saying we throw our hands up and say, "It's all genetic! I'm done caring about the details!" God wants us to care about the details, just as he cares about the details. We are called to teach, love, encourage, discipline, and care for the children entrusted to us.

And I know you're doing the best you can in those areas. I know a lot about you because you are reading this book right now. This is the type of book a great mom would read. I feel confident telling you that you are doing a better job than you realize. You are already providing a wonderful environment for your child to thrive.

I'm here to remind you to exhale. We can relax because every little decision we make isn't always a big deal. We

can arm ourselves with facts to help us remember that the weight of who our kids become isn't all on our shoulders.

The Mindset Shift

We aren't Wonder Women or supermoms—thank goodness, because that would mess up our kids. And we need to get the important things right only half the time.

You won't mess up your kids if they have screen time every day. You know mine were all raised on Nick Jr. and turned out just fine. Avoid any shows with main characters you wouldn't want your kids to imitate, but quality shows that teach positive themes are fine to have on at home so you can take a sanity break.

You won't cause your kids to be overweight because your work schedule doesn't allow time for them to play sports. Research shows that youth sports have no effect on being overweight or obese.[11]

You won't destroy your daughter's health because she won't eat quinoa or vegetables. God made vitamins for a reason.

Your career won't hurt your child unless you choose something awful—pursuing a life as an assassin, for instance. There is no sound body of research showing that women working fulltime is harmful to their children—end of story.

So if how your child turns out is mostly genetics, and you have to get parenting right only 50 percent of the time, then what really matters? **What really matters in the motherhood formula is *you*.** I don't mean the weight of who your child will become rests on you. I mean you being the emotionally healthiest version of you is the best thing you can do for your child.

If you're like me, you want to embrace the idea that you can be more for your kids by doing less. You want to believe the truth that God has already determined who they will become, that he hardwired that into them, and that you can't mess that up. You want to trust the solid research that presents facts to back all that up.

And yet, for some reason, we have a hard time believing God also hardwired *us* to be who we are. He didn't intend for us to be supermoms. He also didn't intend for us to be perfect or to be crushed under the pressure of our expectations. He intended for us to press into who we are and to grow in the strengths *he* gave us as women and as mothers.

You can be more for your kids by doing less.

Remaining you while raising them doesn't mean motherhood won't change you. It will. It means continuing to be who God created you to be while growing and maturing in motherhood.

The magic of motherhood is in who you are, not just what you do.

The good news is that we have agency and can lessen the mother load.

What if we all decided to remove some of that perfectionistic pressure? To lay down some of the weight we carry? Imagine if we decided to do less of some things so we have the ability to enjoy life more?

If you answered three of these with a yes, then you are a normal mom living in the culture of broken modern motherhood. You are in great company. Now let's dive into how to overcome the supermom myth—the myth that good moms can do it all.

How to Overcome the Supermom Myth

1. Don't Believe in the Blank Slate

Our children are not blank slates that we can paint our dreams on. The notion that we can *make* our children turn out the way we want is a lie.

Every child is born with unique DNA (except for identical twins, of course). This unique DNA helps determine how far they will go in certain areas, what they will like, and their personality.

SUPERMOM LIST

Are you at risk of believing the Supermom Myth?

Yes No

- Do you often criticize yourself? ☐ ☐

- If your child struggles, do you think it's your fault? ☐ ☐

- Do you worry you aren't doing enough? ☐ ☐

- Are your high expectations stressing everyone out? ☐ ☐

- Does analysis paralysis cause you to second-guess yourself? ☐ ☐

- Compared with other moms, do you often feel you could do better? ☐ ☐

2. Let Them Make Mistakes

Let your kids make mistakes. In our house, we wanted our kids to make little mistakes when they were young and still living at home. Otherwise, they would go out in the world and get crushed by reality.

- Hurting a friend's feelings helps them learn how to seek and also offer forgiveness.
- Minor illnesses build a great immune system, so it's okay to get dirty and even live by the five-second rule (or, in my sons' case, the five-minute rule).
- Getting sick from too much candy at Easter helps them learn there is such a thing as too much of a good thing.
- Failing a test teaches natural consequences and encourages learning new study habits.

3. Protect Your Sanity

As we discovered, the culture of perfectionism causes parental anxiety, which gives our kids anxiety. You have to protect your sanity. You won't break the cycle until you decide to step away

from the endless advice and fearmongering found online. Yes, with God and Google, all things are possible. But Google is not always a reliable source of information. God doesn't need vetting; Google does. And so do your well-meaning friends and family.

I had to learn to stop going to Facebook and blogs with all the "expert" advice that contradicted itself. I developed a script I would use when someone told me I was doing it wrong. I say, "I understand how you feel. This is how we do it in our family. Thanks for sharing with me." Then I repeat it in various ways until the nosy neighbor or relative who means well stops offering the advice.

Let Them See You

You are doing a wonderful job already. You are discovering what matters, what doesn't matter as much as you thought, and new ways to give yourself grace. I'm proud of you for that.

Just as Luisa in *Encanto* felt she had the world on her shoulders and learned she didn't have to do it all herself, we can too. We don't have to do everything perfectly—we need to do it good enough only half the time—good enough and covered in grace.

Good enough and covered in grace can be perfect.

Our little daily decisions won't mess up our kids. But being too perfect, too demanding, or too anxious can. Let's love our kids well, try to enjoy them even when they drive us crazy, and aim for being good enough and covered in grace. Let them see you mess up, dust yourself off, and make it right. Let them see you love well, even when life is hard. Let them see you make mistakes, make amends, and then carry on with life. Let them see you love yourself enough that you don't feel pressured to be perfect, and love them enough to allow imperfection in them too.

What if those are the most important lessons that can ever be caught? Maybe that is perfect after all.

I Want You to Remember

What if every mistake we make actually helps our children build resilience, tolerance, and empathy? What if this helps our children see that good people sometimes make awful mistakes? This insight will help them understand real life and build their character as they grow and learn.

If we never expose our children to our failures or imperfections, they won't know the first thing about dealing with people in the real world. When we make mistakes, we're teaching our kids how to deal with other imperfect people they'll run into throughout their lives.

The moment we become parents, we are part of a culture that pushes perfectionistic parenting. We are told everything we do matters. We are warned that if we mess up, our children will suffer. The culture of parenting criticism tells us that we are completely responsible for our kids and everything that happens to them. No wonder modern motherhood is crushing us.

More is caught than taught with our kids. That is why we must invest in ourselves and our emotional health.

If anxious overparenting produces fearful kids, then maybe we can free ourselves from the impossible standards that culture has set for us. When we do, our kids have a great shot at being freed from that same anxiety.

Our culture conditions us to believe that our child's personality and future are determined *only* by our actions. The truth is, their personality and future result from a mix of our parenting, their environment, and genetics.

We can wear ourselves out trying to control every little detail of our children's lives. But the truth is that God has encoded them with their own little personalities, strengths, weaknesses, and abilities.

Journal and Discussion

♥ What version of supermotherhood have you been trying to live up to? Which plate will you stop spinning this week? Why that one?

♥ Is it a relief to know that God created your child and that who they become is not all up to you?

♥ How does the mother load and the concept of mental load show up in your life? What are some responsibilities that you could share with others to make your life easier?

♥ You *are* super in some ways. Take some time to think about what you do best. Spend a few minutes listing all the things you are doing well.

PART 3

Habits That Help You Thrive

You now know about the good-mom myths that try to steal your joy. But be aware that they will pop back up and try to weigh you down. Faster than a toddler can spill your coffee, a simple scroll on social media can trigger thoughts of, "Everyone else is doing it better than me. I'm not doing enough."

It's time to replace what has been holding you back with small things that will fill you up.

In part 3 you will discover the power of small habits to transform your life. I know, the word *habits* sounds like code for doing more work. But don't worry, this isn't asking you to do more—you do so much already. We are going to look only at habits that will help you thrive.

Now that the myths are behind us, let's have some fun and look at what can bring you more fulfillment, happiness, and help.

CHAPTER 9

Small Changes, Big Results

Have you ever read a book that changed your life? A book that opened your eyes and helped you see things differently from that point on? (I hope you say that about this one and tell all your friends to read it!) For me, that book was *Atomic Habits*. I saw it on the bestseller lists and tried to ignore it like I ignored the advice to lift weights and eat more salads. Then one day, I gave it a chance.

Atomic Habits taught me that making little changes over time leads to big results. Previously, my strategy for change always ended badly. I tended to decide I would change things, then tackle a big impossible task, get instantly overwhelmed, and give up. God love my sweet family, who has endured this cycle with me many times.

A few years ago, I decided it was time for the whole family to get healthy.

Junk food? Threw it out!

Wake-up time? Five o'clock!

Exercise? Joined a family gym!

On the menu? Lentils and sprouts!

The kids whined and cried, Mark ignored everything, and I was mad at all of them. "I'm just trying to help you," I moaned. No one cared. It was close to a full-on mutiny, resulting in pizza runs behind my back. Bless it.

Turns out that when we decide to reach for a big goal or overhaul something significant in our lives, we go into performance mode. We try to do too much all at once.

Up until reading *Atomic Habits*, I had no idea I was the reason my efforts to change were failing. I was trying to make big, sweeping changes that overwhelmed everyone. **Luckily, I learned the power of making tiny changes that, over time, would add up to big results.**

I have a friend, Maria, a mom of three girls, who joined a marathon group for nonrunning women. When she told me she wanted to run a marathon for her thirtieth birthday, I responded as any good friend would. *"Why?"*

Maria explained that she had always wanted to run one but had failed every time she tried to train for one. She'd had shin splints and a stress fracture in her foot, couldn't figure out how to control her breathing, and had even fainted on one of her runs.

"Let me get this straight," I challenged. "Shin splints, broken bones, and passing out? Again, I ask, *why* do you want to do this?"

But twenty weeks later, she ran a marathon, the whole thing, without stopping. And when I asked her how her training was different, she explained it to me. When she tried to train on her own, she simply got out there and ran. She had zero clue what she was doing but thought the best approach was to run until she couldn't run anymore. By doing that, she wasn't really building up to a marathon. She had a goal, but no incremental steps to get there.

Then she joined the running group, and they started off not by running but by learning what kind of shoes and socks to buy, how to hydrate and fuel their bodies before, during, and after a run, and about cooling and stretching—all things she'd never considered.

Then, on her first real training run, she ran for only thirty seconds and then walked for a minute. She did this over and over and over for a mile. She said at first she thought she'd die, but within a week her running intervals were longer than her walking intervals, and before long she was running miles.

She explained that her slow incremental increases gave her body time to build up strength and stamina. She laughed as she said that she didn't set any records with her marathon time, but that wasn't her goal. Maria's small changes over time made all the difference.

Maria's journey of running the marathon is the perfect illustration of the power of small steps to reach big goals. **It's easy to underestimate how the power of small changes, done repeatedly, can lead to massive results.** I tried to overhaul the way our family lived all at once, and that was a recipe for disaster.

The Power of 1 Percent Better

Setting a big goal and expecting ourselves to accomplish it without small, incremental steps is like waking up one day and deciding you are going to become a lion tamer overnight. It's going to take longer than you think and get messier than you imagine, and you'll definitely get hurt. I learned that the road to success is paved with tiny, easy-to-do habits. I call it the power of 1 percent better.

William Chopik in the Department of Psychology at Michigan State University explains it this way: "The difference a tiny improvement can make over time is astounding. Here's how the math works out. If you can get 1% better each day for one year, you'll end up thirty-seven times better by the time you're done. Conversely, if you get 1% worse each day for one year, you'll decline nearly to zero. What starts as a small win or a minor setback accumulates into something much more."[1]

THE MAGIC OF 1% BETTER

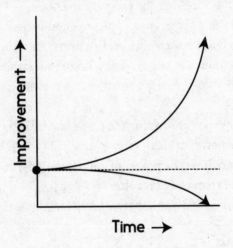

I've never loved math more than I do when I think about the power of 1 percent better!

While overcoming the myth that good moms' kids are obedient and well-behaved, we learned about the importance of looking at life with a long-term view. We learned to think in terms of a child's trajectory, right? This concept applies here too.

The trajectory view and the power of small habits go hand in hand. Sure, your two-year-old had a meltdown at Target because she spilled *one drop* of juice on her baby doll. (Don't worry, it's normal!) But think in terms of progress. Three months ago, she bit the dog and pooped in the bathtub (still normal). Her trajectory is solid, and her habits are improving.

Instead of trying to overhaul my life to get healthier, a better strategy would have been to try to improve 1 percent in an area. Here's how that could look:

Month One—Replace Diet Dr. Pepper with decaf green tea every other day and buy one less junk food item at the store each week.

Month Two—Go for a walk in the evenings (alone if needed) three times a week walking a little faster each time.

Month Three—Cut out the buttered garlic bread and add a little extra vegetables with dinner.

Each change was easy to make because none of these was a huge shock to my system, and they paid off with big results over time.

Our kids learn from our example, and over time our changes will become their inspiration. That inspiration will help them make healthy choices as well. We may never inspire them to trade brownies for brussels sprouts, but **our example will become the benchmark for our kids.**

Habits in the Margins

Is there a mom out there who has a ton of free time? Is anyone lying around eating grapes someone else peeled for her or spending her days getting massages? No way.

We see little fingers slide cars and doll shoes under the door when we pee. We fall asleep at the movies because we are sleep deprived. We balance the mother load—the emotional labor of caring for the family, the house, the pets, and work. We're busier than a one-legged man in a butt-kicking contest.

This is why the power of habits and compounding growth can be a superpower for us. We don't have to do everything all at once; we can make small changes that change our lives over time.

If you can't steal a few hours to read a book, maybe you can read ten pages a day. You would average a book every month. I have a friend, Nina, who reads in the bathtub, and she reads about twenty books a year.

Small habits compound over time for our long-term success.

If you want to learn a new skill, you could buy an online course to use at your own pace or watch YouTube videos for ten minutes a day.

If you want to move your body to boost your happiness but can't get away from the kids, you still have options. You could take your little one in a stroller and challenge the older kids to see who can walk faster between each other.

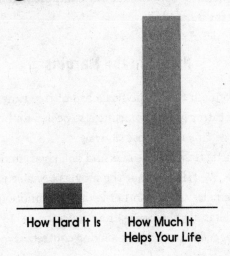

POSITIVE HABITS

How Hard It Is   How Much It Helps Your Life

If you'd like to spend more time with friends but can't get away, use your car line time to phone a friend. Maybe she's in a car line too.

Want to spend less time on social media? Set a daily time limit on your phone for certain apps.

Each of the small habits you incorporate doesn't seem life-altering at the time. But when you take the long view, you can see how life-changing they are.

The Tipping Point

With small habits, we don't see results as fast as we would like, which can trip us up. When I eat sugar snap peas as a snack instead of potato chips, I don't automatically feel healthy and energetic. When I practice breathwork for a week and still feel stressed over little annoyances, I'm tempted to give up. You've been there too, right?

There is a lag between our habits and our results. Building a good habit may not produce results for weeks, months, or even years in some cases. The same is true for bad habits. We may let a bad habit slide because we don't see the negative consequences for a long time. It's easy to ignore the importance of a single decision. But that same decision repeated over and over for months or years can have a massive impact, good or bad.

Atomic Habits has a good metaphor for this concept. Imagine you are flying from Los Angeles to New York City. If the pilot leaving from Los Angeles miscalculates by 3.5 degrees south, then you won't land in New York at all. You'll get off that plane in Washington, DC. No one would notice right away that anything was off course, but in a few hours everyone would be hundreds of miles from their destination.

Slight changes in our daily habits work that way too.

Your work, your relationships, and your choices are never wasted or in vain. The work you do to change yourself does make a difference. Bit by bit, you absorb these new habits, and so do your kids!

We don't have a toaster, thanks to a son who almost burned down our house. Because of what I can only guess is toast-induced PTSD, we never replaced it. We are an overtoasting kind of family.

I make eggs and toast every morning for the kids before school, and I burn the toast no less than once a week. I've made peace with the fact that this is my signature cooking method.

Here's what happens: I put the toast on the baking sheet and place it under the broiler. I check it every thirty seconds or so, and *the bread never changes*. I think I have time to walk to the sink for ten seconds, then I come back, open the oven door, and—voila!—the toast is burnt like a marshmallow dropped in a campfire.

The bread looks normal over and over and over, and then suddenly it's burnt to a crisp.

Our habits can feel that way. We make small changes and repeat a new way of thinking or behavior over and over. It seems like nothing is changing until, like magic, it does.

The tipping point is where the magic is. This phenomenon is known as the tipping point, and the tipping point is where the magic is.

The toast is heating up all the time but looks no different until it hits the tipping point, and in an instant, bread becomes toast.

The same is true of developing new habits. We make the same small changes day after day, and it looks like nothing is happening. We expect our results to be clear and to come quickly. But the results are always delayed, which can send us spiraling into disappointment. It's like training for a marathon. For weeks, it seems like every mile you run is a struggle. You think to yourself,

THE TIPPING POINT

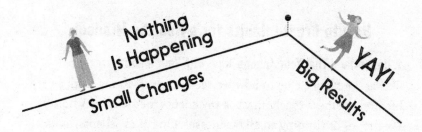

"I'm never going to be able to run." Then suddenly one day you get out there and run, and it's like you've been doing it your whole life.

The work you put in wasn't wasted, it was stored. It seemed like you weren't making progress, but the day comes when you realize the full value of all your effort.[2]

The idea of small things adding up is a perfect way to encapsulate motherhood. All your work, your love, your sacrifices, your choices, your middle-of-the-night hugs, your kind words, your attention—you put in so much work for what seem like minimal results *at the time.* You just hope you are doing it right and that your kids will turn out great.

Don't focus on the messes, the tears, or the fights. Focus on your child's trajectory.

The good news is motherhood is not decided in three or thirty dramatic moments but in thousands and thousands of little moments over time. (And remember, the best part is that we have to get it right only half the time.)

The next few chapters will be about key habits to help you thrive as a mom. First, let's dive into how to build small habits that will bring you big results.

Now, if you're like me and feel like you haven't ever had good luck creating good habits, don't worry; that's not your fault. No one does until they learn the system, which is both simple and powerful.

How to Create Habits for a Healthy Mindset

1. Understand That Your Actions Align with Your Identity

Our actions are a clue to how we see ourselves. In my work as a life and business coach, most of my clients are mothers who are executives or running small businesses. One of my clients, Julia, called me early on a Wednesday morning for help. She wanted more customers. I recommended she get out in the community, meet people, network, and build relationships with other businesses in town.

The more that other people and businesses sent people her way, the faster she would see her sales increase. Easy, right? People have been growing their businesses that way for hundreds of years.

Not for Julia. "Alli, I can't do it. I'm terrible with people. *I'm not that kind of person.*"

The idea of her building a new habit of reaching out to or meeting other business owners didn't align with how she saw herself. She saw herself as shy and awkward. She told herself she wasn't the kind of woman who could go network in the community.

How you see yourself directly affects your behavior.

How we see ourselves sometimes affects our behavior more than we realize. If someone invited me out for a jog, I would say, "No thanks. I'm not a runner." If you see yourself as a runner, you would happily jump right in.

Julia's belief that she was shy and awkward came from being told that when she was younger, and she took that identity to

BEHAVIORS THAT DON'T ALIGN WITH YOUR IDENTITY EITHER WON'T HAPPEN, OR IF THEY DO, THEY WON'T LAST.

heart. It took time to help her see that she was great with people already. She was actively involved in the PTO at her daughter's school (that could have been a full-time job managing people in itself). Hundreds of customers came through her door daily, and she loved chatting with them.

For most of her life she had been telling herself the story that she wasn't good with people. So building a new habit of getting out and meeting new people felt impossible. But when she told herself a new story, things changed. She told herself that she was already great with people because she had the evidence that she was. And once she started behaving out of that identity, her confidence and customers spiked.

Julia had to *change her beliefs before she could change her behavior.* Behaviors that don't align with our identity won't happen, or if they do, they won't last.

Julia decided she wanted to be the type of person who felt comfortable going out and meeting new people. She joined a neighborhood bunco group of twelve women that met one night a month. She signed up for a book club with a friend that met every other month. In both cases, she reminded herself that she was building the habit of making time to go out and meet new people. She took small steps with low commitment, which led to successfully building this new habit into her life.

Julia's habits now align with the belief that she is great at meeting new people, and her business shows it.

2. Focus on Who You Want to Become

My attempt to transform my family into the pinnacle of health was destined to fail from the beginning. I tried to force my ideas on everyone else against their will. I tried to do it all much too fast.

The biggest problem was that I didn't see myself as a healthy person. I saw myself as unhealthy, someone who would never have energy again. I was a girl who much preferred a candy bar and venti latte to a meal with one iota of health benefits. I saw myself as someone who was so exhausted from work and raising kids that all I wanted was to eat some doughnuts and binge-watch *The Crown.*

Now, there's nothing wrong with an occasional TV binge, drinking coffee, or eating doughnuts. I would never say that. It's when those things are habitual and you see yourself in a negative light that making a change in your behavior is harder.

For me, I decided to be healthier, not because I wanted to lose weight or look different but because I wanted to feel good again. I wanted to have energy and still be able to walk around an amusement park. I wanted to spend an active day with my boys without feeling like I was dying.

I wanted to feel healthier, and the only way to do that was to start making small changes.

"What would a healthy person do in this situation?" was my thought when I wanted to stay up until three in the morning watching movies instead of getting a good night's sleep. That one question made me carry my behind to bed so I would have energy the next day and not feel like I was run over by a dump truck.

That one simple question also helped me learn to drink a lot of water, eat my veggies, sleep more, and embrace moving my body to create more energy. I live by the 80/20 rule. Eighty percent of the time, I make healthy decisions. Twenty percent of the time, I make fun choices, like eating pretzels and sunflower seed butter by the spoonful and watching late-night movies with the family.

Over the years, my health journey did influence my family for the better. My husband brought home a dozen doughnuts today as a treat, but we no longer keep them stocked in the pantry. Little changes don't mean we have to deprive ourselves.

3. Give Yourself Proof

We all tell ourselves stories about who we are and what we can or can't do. Sometimes, as in Julia's case, the stories come from harsh words that were said to us. Sometimes, as in my case, the stories come from years of living with ourselves. I lived with myself for forty-five years; I had *proof* that I was unhealthy.

Maybe you want to develop the habit of becoming organized, but you have proof that you are unorganized and messy. You can change the story you tell yourself by giving yourself *new proof*. That proof comes from taking small steps to change your behavior. You create a new habit and clean your car every weekend, braving the old chicken nuggets and juice box straws in the back seat. Then when you see that clean back seat, you give yourself proof that you are organized.

Small Steps = Proof = Long-Term Change

Or you start a new habit of preparing for the next day. You take five minutes each night to write down the next day's most important things and what steps you need to take to accomplish them. This lets you stay ahead of the game and mentally get ahead of the next day. Again, new proof that you are organized.

Maybe you develop a habit of ordering household items on subscription so you never have to remind yourself to get toilet paper or dog food at the last minute. Voila! More proof that you are, in fact, an organized person.

You could even set up a habit with your best friend, selecting one Sunday afternoon every month and alternating houses to tackle an organizing project together. *Girl, look at you. You are swimming in proof.*

Change doesn't happen overnight, but when you decide who you want to become and then build in small habits, you will give yourself enough proof to wake up one day and say, "What do you know? I am an organized person!"

Think of life like a big progress bar. The little steps you take are progress. Our mindset shifts to the trajectory in our life and our child's trajectory instead of the hassles, hang-ups, and heartaches of the day.

We are on our way to our target destination; all we have to do is stay on course with little steps in the right direction.

I Want You to Remember

Remember the power of 1 percent better. If you can get 1 percent better each day for one year, you'll end up thirty-seven times better at the end of that year. If you get 1 percent worse each day for one year, you'll decline to zero.

The tipping point is where all your small steps and changes build up and suddenly you see the results of your effort.

Your habits are a clue to how you see yourself. How you see yourself directly affects your behavior. Behaviors that don't align with your identity won't happen, or if they do, they won't last.

You can change the story you tell yourself by giving yourself new proof. That proof comes from taking small steps to change your behavior. Small Steps = Proof = Long-Term Change.

Think of life like a big progress bar. The little steps you take are progress. Our mindset shifts to our trajectory in life and our child's trajectory instead of the hassles, hangups, and heartaches of the day.

Journal and Discussion

♥ Have you ever thought about how your identity guides your behavior? What does it look like in your life?

♥ What changes have you hoped to make but have given up on because you couldn't do it all at once?

♥ You have a list of things you wish were different. We all do. How do the changes you want to make align with your identity, and how will you prioritize those changes?

♥ What is one area in which are you looking for large-scale change? What incremental steps can you take, starting today, to make that change a reality?

CHAPTER 10

The Magic Question Habit

Growing up, I watched the women on one side of my family host massive holiday gatherings. They cooked for days. How do I know they cooked for days? They told me, they told my cousins, they told the cat, they told everyone, repeatedly, all day long. Even as a girl in elementary school, I noticed the subtle undercurrent of bitterness in their voices.

Why did they do all that work and get so mad about it?

If I cooked a massive meal that took me days to prepare (which, for the record, I would never do because I don't cook. I'm a slow-cooker chef. Mark makes all the holiday meals in our house because we don't want food poisoning . . . I digress, but *if* I did), you'd better believe I would tell everyone and smile and wait for their undying gratitude.

It wasn't the women's telling everyone about their cooking that I noticed; it was the bitterness. At eight years of age, I didn't have the life experience or language to understand what was happening. But I did know there was something wrong. And even as a young girl, I knew that whatever it was, I didn't want to replicate it in my life.

Age and experience gave me the perspective to look back on my core memories with new understanding. As adults, we can unpack our memories with empathy for the people involved. I now see that the women in my family felt pressured to cook and host these massive holiday gatherings. The women in my family watched with genuine happiness as their extended families ate and relaxed. At the same time, they also desperately needed some help in the kitchen and some appreciation for all the work they had done.

Great-Aunt Shirley didn't feel like she had permission to ask for what she needed. I found out after she passed that she didn't even want to cook all those meals. She would have preferred to have everyone bring a dish and relax. She felt pressure (real or imagined) to do everything herself. Through the years, Shirley became increasingly bitter watching her family have a blast, while she sat exhausted from days of preparation.

Eight-year-old Alli knew something was wrong, and she knew she didn't want that in her life. As an adult, I decided early on that no amazing holiday meal, or any other massive undertaking I don't really want to take on, is worth making myself miserable. Nothing is worth sending bitter vibes to my family all day. I've said it before, and I'll say it again: if mama ain't happy, ain't nobody happy.

Permission to Do What Works for You

On a whim, thirty years later, I wrote an article embracing what I called slacker parenting. It was a response to the overparenting that so many women felt pressured to do.

I asked,

What if instead of hovering over your kids at night, making sure every last math problem is correct, and every book report is finished . . . you simply didn't . . . and let them learn to do their work? What if your morning routine of running around making sure the kids are dressed and all their lunches are packed no longer was your problem? And you just let them pick out their clothes and, get this, pack their own lunches? Of course, you may have to step in and draw the line somewhere. Otherwise, they'd probably walk off with their pants on backward and Cap'n Crunch sandwiches for lunch. But, for the most part, think of all the extra time you'd have. You could take a whole 10-minute-long shower!

"Slacker parenting" was my tongue-in-cheek way of saying that parents have permission to focus on the majors, not the minors. Not every little thing has to be perfect. And we can choose to give ourselves grace, permission not to run ourselves ragged. I'm not talking about neglecting our children. I'm talking about moms who never err on the side of doing too little; we do too much. When we constantly overfunction, we need permission to breathe and get some perspective.

The article went live, and I waited for the masses of judgy moms to show up at my online door with pitchforks. The pitchforks never arrived. Instead, a *Good Morning America* producer emailed me. They had a local crew in Nashville and wanted to talk about slacker parenting. Six hours later, they were in my living room filming a segment on how I parented.

Think about it for a second—we had a *six-hour* warning. My house was brimming with kid stuff, overrun with backpacks and sports equipment. And dog hair covered 90 percent of it. We scooped up the clutter that graced the tables, floors, and countertops and put it into large plastic bins. I made peace with the fact that dog hair *probably* wouldn't show up on camera. My main comfort was that at least I would be true to the message I was preaching—it doesn't have to be perfect to be great.

Good Morning America filmed my elementary schooler loading the dishes and the boys playing Legos, all with a preschooler jumping on a little indoor trampoline in our dining room. And like an out-of-body experience, I found myself on national TV talking about what I believed was and wasn't important in parenting.

My husband and I talked about helping our kids grow up able to give and receive love. We discussed helping them take personal responsibility for themselves. And we dove into the importance of developing self-confidence through household responsibilities. And most importantly, we agreed that these things do not happen when we do everything for our kids.

Moms, therapists, and teachers inundated me with thanks for giving women permission to live their lives and parent in a way that worked for them. Being a slacker mom was a silly way to give women permission to do what's right for them and their families. **We don't have to play by anyone else's rules or live up to their expectations.** Certainly not the "rules" that say women must cook for days for a holiday to be happy or valuable. Nor the ones that say moms must throw the most elaborate Pinterest birthday parties ever recorded in social media history. Let's trash the one that says our kids must look perfect and always behave. Or that those same kids must sit and do homework for hours every night because they have to be on the honor roll.

After I came out as a slacker mom on national TV, my conversations with other moms changed. Instead of small talk, they launched right into their struggles and issues. I discovered one of the biggest issues we have as moms is not what we think it is. It isn't trying to curate a perfect childhood or making sure we meet every need our children have.

Our biggest issue is asking ourselves what *we* need.

"What do I need?" is the magic question that will guide you in how to care for yourself and your family in a way that gives you confidence and freedom.

Great-Aunt Shirley needed to feel like she had permission to sit down and enjoy her family during holidays and tell everyone to bring a dish. Shirley needed to know she was still valued and a great mom even if she didn't perform.

Many of us have seen women in our families put themselves last. We watched them ignore their emotional health and suffer because of it. We never had a concept of what taking care of ourselves looked like. And we never learned to give ourselves permission to take care of ourselves.

The Power of Asking the Magic Question: What Do I Need?

The magic question allows you to focus on what matters. It allows you to model healthy behaviors for your kids. And you can protect yourself from letting motherhood make you feel like a victim.

From the moment we find out we will become a mom, we naturally focus on what the child needs. But we must also learn to ask for what we need. If we don't, our needs get left on the shelf and our emotional health pays the price.

As we mother our children, we need to mother ourselves too. Most of the time, we can figure out what our children need and then meet those needs. But we can't always figure out what we need. As we learn to mother ourselves, we can discover what we need. Then we can find the best way to meet that need.

Asking yourself what you need is part of mothering yourself. Mothering yourself allows you to mother others well.

As I built the habit of asking myself, "What do I need?" I became more comfortable identifying what I needed and advocating for it.

Here's a list of what I needed.

1. I Needed More Help around the House

The reality—My husband is not someone who cleans like I do. He handles driving the kids to school and their appointments, most of the cooking, and the outside chores. He also breaks down the gazillion cardboard boxes I throw in the garage every week, He has many wonderful gifts, and he is my biggest encourager. But he will not divide all household chores with me on a regular basis. I've made peace with that.

I tell you this because the division of household labor is a big issue. Most online advice givers seem to assume husbands will hear about their wife's desire for them to do more and then magically jump right in and do everything she asks. That's great for some, but it isn't always the case.

In chapter 12, I'm going to share that 69 percent of marital conflict never gets resolved. Some husbands won't change in certain areas. That's okay. It's good to live in the real world and get some comfort from the fact that nothing is perfect.

How I took care of my needs—Once the kids were early elementary age, they could unload and load the dishwasher. While they learned, I packed up all the nice dishes and glasses. I gave the kids more and more jobs as they grew older—laundry, garbage, mowing, vacuuming. They don't get an allowance for their work. They are part of a family, and family members have responsibilities.

I also realized that a housekeeper is cheaper than a divorce (I'm kidding . . . sort of), so as soon as my business brought in the income for it, I hired a housekeeper.

2. I Needed to Make My Life Easier

The reality—Don't we all need to make our lives easier? Life is already hard enough. We all juggle more than humans were meant to do every day. Work, doctor appointments, mountains of never-ending, soul-crushing laundry, groceries, paying the bills, cooking, did anyone feed the cat?—there's a lot going on. The mother load weighs a million pounds.

WHAT DO I NEED?

Less Social Media

Housekeeper

Sleep

Less Family Drama

More Sex

More Energy

A Day Off

Time to Build My Faith

How I took care of my needs—I started with the little things around my house. I created systems to manage the mental load (as a gift, at the end of this book, you'll get a guide to building systems to help out with the mother load), I had groceries delivered, and we ate the same meals on rotation every week. I told the boys no video games or TV until they had done their homework and packed their lunches for the next day. And no, I didn't check on this. I took their word for it. And yes, sometimes they lied and learned not to mess around and lie to Mom. I quit buying junk food to limit food battles in the house. We now go out for junk but don't keep it in the cabinet.

3. I Needed More Energy

The reality—I was flat-out tired. I would love to take a nap during the day, but I always woke up feeling like I didn't know who I was or where I was, so it wasn't worth it. Coffee upset my stomach, so that wasn't an answer, but I was so exhausted. I couldn't even remember what it felt like to have energy.

How I took care of my needs—Small changes over time gave me the energy I needed. I started moving my body a little more. I drank my body weight in decaf green tea (which nutritionally counts as water) because water is gross. I put a sleep tracker on my watch and made sure I got at least seven hours of sleep every night. I started taking vitamin D supplements after my annual physical showed I was low. I began to move more and get exercise. Simple small steps over time added up to the energy I needed.

4. I Needed to Stop Falling into the Comparison Trap

The reality—I want a spotless house that's gorgeous and well-decorated. I also wish all my family members were well-dressed like we just popped out of a Ralph Lauren advertisement. I want to go on adventures on the weekends and have big, multifamily get-togethers. But my life doesn't look that way. With two boys with chronic migraines, we don't do loud things. Another son has Asperger's, and asking him to spend his downtime with more groups of people is torture. My goal is to balance my needs with the needs of those I love.

How I take care of my needs—I remind myself that this is the wonderful life God has given me. It's not perfect, but it's pretty great, and being a wife and mom is my greatest joy. Most importantly, I decided to limit my time on social media, especially the kind with photos and videos of people I've never met. I'm going to be real with you. Nothing makes me feel worse than watching families I've never met document their best lives while I'm struggling to get through the grind of the day. No thank you. I'll pass.

Pro tip—I unfollowed the accounts that triggered dissatisfaction in me. I decided to follow accounts that aren't full of selfies and staged family photos. The accounts I love to follow now are my real friends and accounts that encourage, educate, or entertain me. When I scroll social media, I see my good friends, baby sea otter videos, and posts where I can learn something. That makes me happy.

Most of us go to social media to feel connected to others, but research shows that the more we scroll, the worse we feel afterward. Passively scrolling and looking at everyone's highlight reels, subconsciously comparing them to our daily reality, is a recipe for dissatisfaction. But we can use social media in a healthy way if we use it to connect with our friends and to pour into our real friendships. We'll do a deep dive on this in chapter 13!

5. I Needed to Feel More Fulfilled

The reality—Most of life isn't fulfilling. Life is paying bills and cleaning the carpet after your dog eats a sock and throws up.

There's way too much fishing poop out of a toddler's bathtub. No one wants to have to ground a teenager for lying. And there is a surprising amount of making Crock-Pot chili because, gracious, does this family ever stop eating? It's not a recipe for feeling amazing and fulfilled every day.

How I take care of my needs—Research confirmed what I have experienced to be true: having a deep sense of faith leads to a more fulfilling life.[1] My relationship with God is the most fulfilling thing in my life. My family brings me deep joy and happiness, but my relationship with God gives my life meaning and purpose.

> My family brings me deep joy and happiness, but my relationship with God gives my life meaning and purpose.

My work as a life and business coach is also fulfilling. I get to invest in women's lives and help them as they navigate life and build their careers and their businesses. And, of course, my relationships are fulfilling. Prioritizing my relationships with Mark and good friends helps me feel like I'm living life to the fullest.

What Do You Need?

I asked my friends and clients to start practicing the habit of asking the magic question. Most of them gave me a variation of the same answer: "I have no idea what I need, and I don't have time to figure it out."

Asking yourself what you need can feel so big, almost like the answer carries the weight of your entire future.

I refined the question a little and asked, "What do you need *right now*?" Even with that nuance, many struggled. But little by little, when they felt lost and overwhelmed, they became accustomed to stopping and asking, "What do I need right now?"

Caroline shared that she needed only one thing in this season of life—more sleep. Her toddler was waking up in the middle of the night, and her preschooler woke up at four o'clock in the morning happily screeching, "Mooom!" Her husband had left and filed for divorce six months earlier, so she had no relief. Caroline got creative and rented her spare bedroom to a college student who was getting her child and family studies degree. In

Asking "What do I need right now?" is a smart first step in getting your needs met.

exchange for a teeny portion of rent, Caroline's new roommate helped with dinner prep, laundry, and the early morning shift with the kids so Caroline could sleep until six. Caroline said that sleeping those extra two hours was the best thing she did for her mental health in that painful first year as a single mom.

Chantal shared that she needed to establish boundaries in her relationship with her mother and sister. Her family was overly dramatic about everything. They felt life fully and loved to discuss every detail. Chantal found herself exhausted by it while trying to keep up with daily work demands and parenting two sons. She told her mom and sister that she couldn't talk for a long time every day and couldn't be expected to reply to everything in the family group chat. It was awkward, to say the least, but she set those boundaries and was healthier for it.

Elizabeth reported back that she needed to have more sex. She and her husband were exhausted with their kids. By the time they crawled into bed every night, they were interested in sex but too tired to do anything about it. Her answer was, "Why wait until bedtime?" One night she marched into the living room after putting the twin toddlers to bed and said, "Jason, I need your hands on me. Who says we have to wait until bedtime? Let's go, buddy." His reaction was priceless. Elizabeth told me he had never jumped up to respond to a communicated need faster.

My coaching client, Olivia, started asking herself the magic question. After about two weeks, she realized she needed to stop automatically taking people's opinions as fact. I developed a list of questions that Olivia now asks herself when she decides if an opinion has merit in her life.

- Does this opinion have weight and meaning for me?
- Does this person care about me and have my best interests at heart?
- Do they know the facts well enough to give this opinion?
- Do they have enough experience with this situation to give them expertise?
- Do they have their own pain or ongoing issues that give them a skewed perspective?
- Does their life reflect characteristics I want to replicate in mine?

Does this opinion have merit?

Kylie needed her husband to take on more of the responsibilities she was carrying. She explained that she needed help because she felt like she was drowning under the mother load. She and her husband laid out all the tasks that needed to be done every week and decided together who would own each one. Deciding together helped make sure no one felt attacked or pushed into taking on a responsibility under pressure. I encouraged Kylie and her husband to meet every six months to assess the system: Were all tasks getting done? Do any changes need to happen? This way their communication stays open so both of them can get their needs met.

Rachel needed to have some time to herself other than when her school-aged kids were asleep. She needed time when she wouldn't hear "Honey, do you know where this is?" or the "Mom, can you make Matt stop bothering me?" type of questions. It was as if her family waited to interrupt her when she tried to sit out on her deck and enjoy a cup of tea and a good book. Her husband said a couple of hours a week was totally doable and agreed to take their kids (and dog) to the local dog park every Saturday for two hours.

Learning to ask ourselves what we need and then discovering how to meet those needs can feel awkward at first. We aren't used to having our needs met. But figuring out what we need *right now* is a great small step toward caring for ourselves and our mental health.

Real Talk

Motherhood has a million moments when we may feel like we have no control over anything.

There are moments when all you need is a nap, but the baby is wide awake and forces you to carry her around to keep her from wailing.

There are moments when you need to sit and cry, but your toddler demands you sit on the floor with him and pretend to be a fire truck anyway.

There are moments when you get stuck at the pediatrician's office for a well checkup and have to wait hours. You wonder if it's worth it to leave and come back another time, but you've already waited so long. Surely you must be next. You start dreaming up escape plans like a scene from *The Shawshank Redemption*.

There are moments when you need to pee so badly, but the baby is asleep in her car seat in the back seat. If you wake her up, she will be a disaster all afternoon. So you continue driving around in misery, hoping you won't wet your pants.

Yes, sometimes our circumstances rule the day, but those

should be the exception and not the rule. My great-aunt Shirley lived a good part of her life feeling like a victim to her role in the family and the norms she thought she had to live up to. No one ever told her she had permission to ask the magic question and change things for herself.

I'm so sorry if no one has ever told you that you have permission. I want you to hear it from me now. It is good and healthy to get in touch with how you feel and discover what you need. And it is 100 percent okay to ask for your needs to be met.

God tells us he will meet all our needs.[2] **Not only does that mean it is okay to have needs, it is also okay to ask for them to be met. God meets our needs in many ways, including through the people in our lives.**

The magic question will not only help you survive motherhood, it will also help you thrive in light of the promise that God sees your needs and supplies them.

PERMISSION GRANTED

- [ ] Do what's right for you.
- [ ] Breathe and get perspective.
- [ ] Live and parent by your values.
- [ ] Take care of yourself.
- [ ] Protect your boundaries.

I Want You to Remember

"What do I need?" is the magic question that will guide you in how to care for yourself and your family in a way that gives you confidence and freedom. Asking yourself what you need is part of mothering yourself. Mothering yourself allows you to mother others well.

How to decide if an opinion has merit:

- Does this opinion have weight and meaning for me?
- Does this person care about me and have my best interests at heart?
- Do they know the facts well enough to give this opinion?
- Do they have enough experience with this situation to give them expertise?
- Do they have their own pain or ongoing issues that give them a skewed perspective?
- Does their life reflect characteristics I want to replicate in mine?

You have permission to:

- Do what's right for you.
- Breathe and get perspective.
- Live and parent by your values.
- Take care of yourself.
- Protect your boundaries.

Journal and Discussion

♥ What do you need right now? Don't overthink it. See what pops into your head.

♥ Who can help take some pressure off you in terms of your mental load? A husband, housekeeper, or babysitter? If you had a magic wand and could magically get the help you need, where would you start?

♥ Have you ever experienced disappointment or bitterness because of years of not having your needs met? What small step you can take today to mother yourself and help protect yourself from feeling like that in the future?

CHAPTER 11

The Power of a
Great Soundtrack

A marble jar convinced me I was failing as a mother. It was a Saturday afternoon, and I was minding my business watching YouTube videos trying to fix an issue I had with my website. YouTube then suggested a video for parents about how to savor the time they have left with their children. As if when the kids graduate high school, we stop contact and move on with life as if we never knew each other.

In the video, a kind man showed a jar of 936 marbles, each marble representing a week of my child's life from birth to high school graduation. The goal was to remove a marble a week and let it remind me to savor the time I had with each child, to use my time as a mother wisely. All while keeping in mind that my time with my children was *dwindling*.

I bought the jar and all the marbles. I wanted to be a "good mom," and this seemed like a great way to keep myself on track. The jar sat in my kitchen, and as I removed marbles, week by week, my thoughts spiraled.

Did I do enough?

Did I teach them enough?

Did I create lasting "good" memories?

Did I spend enough quality time with them?

Did I tell them about how much God loves them?

Well, another marble, another wasted week that I can't get back.

Do you know what that jar became to me? A colorful visual reminder to beat myself up. I fell into the trap of believing I was supposed to do everything right all the time. I had to teach them everything they needed to know. I needed to instill my values and dreams in them. On top of that, I needed to do it all before they graduated from high school.

Each colorful little marble was an added weight on my shoulders.

Guilt. Worry. Pressure. Fear.

My stupid marble jar and I shared a kitchen for ten weeks, until my friend Pamela dropped by one day and noticed it. She is a brilliant woman and is oh so wise. She is always well put together and never has an unkind word for anyone. When she asked about the jar, I launched into the story in the most cheerful, upbeat way. I wanted to say all the right things. I explained how it helped me to use my time well and to remember that my time with the kids was limited, and I wanted to steward it well.

MY STUPID MARBLE JAR

I waited for her to be impressed with what an intentional mother I was. I just knew she would tell me I was doing a good job. Pamela listened and then snorted. She snort-laughed at me! She didn't even try to hold it in.

"Alli, that sounds like a recipe to make mothers feel miserable."

Without missing a beat, I blurted, "It is. I hate it so much!"

She shared that a tool like a marble jar may work for some moms who love the reminder. For other (and possibly most) women, it would trigger guilt and worry and unleash a cascade of shame-filled thoughts that tell us we are doing it wrong.

"Alli, never take *all* parenting advice to heart. The marble jar is not for you. And for that matter, never take parenting advice from anyone who doesn't have grown children. Everyone is an expert when their kids are under ten."

Turns out, we don't have to teach our kids everything they need to know by the time they turn eighteen. We couldn't if we wanted to. Oh, the internet would like to convince you that you can and should, but you can't. The articles, books, and classes out there telling us to savor every moment, create a legacy of memories, and enjoy our kids while they are little—all that advice can set us up to feel terrible about ourselves while we are in the exhausting years of motherhood.

As we may have suspected, there's no one right way to do anything, only what is right for you and each child, individually. The internet does not always know what is right for *your* baby, and for that matter, neither does Great-Aunt Sarah, Nancy the Neighbor, or baby book bestsellers.

> There's no one right way to do anything, only what is right for you and each child, individually.

Who best knows your baby's needs? You do. You can raise your children with confidence, knowing their needs better than anyone else because you know your children better than anyone else.

Pamela had four adult children ages twenty-two to thirty-four. She shared that she taught them many of the most important life lessons long after they left for college.

Fast-forward a decade, and I've lived out the truth she gave me that day with my own grown children. I don't give them wisdom, advice, and help daily when they are grown-ups. But when big things happen in life and they need wise counsel, I'm there.

We may want to teach our children lessons they won't be psychologically or biologically ready to learn until they have been out of the house for years. But you don't have to do it all before they walk into adulthood. It's impossible to teach kids everything they need to know before their brains are done developing. In fact, your child's brain will continue maturing until their midtwenties. The last areas to develop are skills such as planning, prioritizing, and controlling impulses.[1] There's a reason car insurance rates don't go down until drivers are twenty-five!

Sometimes we get the best-*sounding* advice, but it's actually the worst.

For example:

Enjoy them now before they are teenagers.

>It's hard to hear that while your toddler and preschooler are punching each other and fighting to the death over a pack of fruit snacks. Whenever someone told me to enjoy them while they were little, all I thought was, "You mean it gets worse?"

You'll miss these days.

>I get it. Babies are cute. They also don't sleep, they poop on you, and their ability to time their projectile vomiting to the precise moment you are leaving the house is unnerving. And toddlers are adorable with their little mispronounced words like *Double boo* (*W*), *packpack* (*backpack*), and *rockamole* (*guacamole*). I loved the toddler phase when I was in it. But I have never once missed the toddler phase now that I'm enjoying

joking around with my teens, seeing a movie together, or spending all day at a theme park. My son James and I now have the goal of riding every massive roller coaster in the country together. In the last three years, we've been to twelve parks, braved the biggest coasters, eaten our body weight in snacks, and had an absolute blast. I'll take teens over toddlers any day.

Blink and they'll be grown.

On some difficult days, I have blinked as fast as humanly possible. My crazy toddlers grew into rowdy boys; messy, moody teenagers; and then know-it-all young adults. I loved them at every stage, but there were definitely days I would have blinked straight to the next stage.

What if we put away our laundry lists of things we feel pressured to teach? Instead, let's focus on enjoying our kids and taking great care of ourselves. Let's spend time providing a home where deep relationships (and eventually friendships) will grow. This is where the habit of having healthy thoughts comes in.

The Power of Our Thoughts

Remember the old digital photo frame in our kitchen? The story of us? All I saw were the messes, and I beat myself up over the things that weren't perfect. But the rest of the family saw happy memories and laughs and ridiculous antics.

We lived out those memories together, but how we thought about those memories created the soundtracks we played about them. I had to learn to see those memories through their eyes and change my thoughts about the story of us. It's amazing that simply changing my thoughts changed my memories.

Broken Soundtracks

Most of us have soundtracks that play on repeat that we picked up in childhood from adults in our lives. Many of those soundtracks are ones we heard our moms play to themselves. Generations of women have been burdened with the soundtracks they heard, internalized, and then played themselves.

In *Encanto*, the grandmother, Abuela Alma Madrigal, suffers horrible trauma. As a young mother of triplets, she is displaced from her home and sees her husband murdered. A miracle happens after her husband's death. Alma, her triplet babies, and the other displaced community members are set in the middle of a city closed off from the outside world. A magical house, Casita, appears for Alma and her children. Alma sees herself and her family as the keeper of the miracle and protector of the community. In Alma's pain, she strives to make everything in her new community perfect.

Alma suffered trauma. Then she passed down her internal soundtrack to "be perfect" to her children and grandchildren and, as a result, created something known as generational trauma. Generational trauma is a pattern of thoughts and behaviors that happens because of a traumatic experience. This pattern is passed down to younger generations who never directly experienced the trauma themselves.

My friend Lee shared with me that her mother's broken soundtrack was about how horrible being a mother was. Her mother often said things like, "You kids are driving me crazy. I don't know why I had you when all you do is get on my last nerve." Then in Lee's presence, her mother would complain to other moms that she needed to get away from her "monsters" before they made her lose her mind.

Of course, Lee internalized those soundtracks and spent

her twenties wondering if being a mother was for her. After her thirtieth birthday, she discovered that her grandmother had died in childbirth. Her mother grew up hearing from her father that she had *killed her mother*. Lee had a new understanding that her mother had suffered the trauma of hearing a damaging broken soundtrack. Her mother passed that trauma on to her with her words.

At thirty-two, Lee had her first baby. Thanks to prayer and a lot of therapy, she made sure the broken soundtrack her mother played stopped with her generation.

Lee discovered that what she heard growing up wasn't a reflection of her worth as a person, but rather it was her mother's generational pain coming through. It wasn't her fault, and she did not deserve it. *She couldn't make that distinction as a child, but it was crucial for her healing to make the distinction as an adult.*

After Lee identified the broken soundtrack, she was able to replace it with the truth. Her new soundtrack is "I am wonderfully made and a wonderful mom."

Much like Alma's children and grandchildren, Lee had what experts call a legacy burden. **Legacy burdens are beliefs, emotions, and thought patterns passed down through generations.** Legacy burdens are the result of generational trauma.

Legacy burdens aren't from your own life experience. They are formed and transmitted to us through someone else's experience, not from our own. Legacy burdens show up in our automatic thoughts and feelings about the world. They will *feel* true to us even if we've never had the experience of them being true.

Some families pass down beliefs like the following:

- People will always try to hurt you.
- You must always look good and make others happy with you.

- Working hard and saving money is the most important thing you can do as an adult.
- Putting your needs first is selfish.

Alma's family members each bore the legacy burden from her trauma as well as a unique magical gift. (Remember how strong Luisa was? She lifted all those donkeys!) The burden, combined with the gift, left each family member full of anxiety and under pressure to perform and be perfect. The gift they each had was there to serve the community. And the star of the story, young Mirabel, was the first descendant without a gift.

LEGACY BURDENS ARE THE RESULT OF GENERATIONAL TRAUMA.

Mirabel, without the pressure of a gift, was the one who was free enough to see that something was broken and unhealthy in her family. She showed her abuela Alma compassion for what she had been through, and she also showed her there was a better, healthier way to live.

Encanto is a beautiful movie full of broken soundtracks. Likewise, some of us have beautiful lives with broken motherhood soundtracks. **We've debunked five good-mom myths**

together, myths that are nothing more than soundtracks passed from mom to mom.

Good moms put their families first.
Good moms' kids are obedient and well-behaved.
Good moms don't get angry.
Good moms protect their children from pain.
Good moms can do it all.

Those are the broken soundtracks we have listened to as moms. And in replaying them over and over, we internalized them, believing them to be true, and we have carried the weight of them as shame and guilt.

But we have also learned the power of speaking new soundtracks over old myths.

Good moms can put their families first by putting themselves first. By prioritizing yourself, you are doing your best for your family. So when you walk out the door to go to work, you say, "Good moms go to work at jobs they love." And if you enjoy a girls' night out, you say, "Good moms build deep friendships and spend quality time with their friends." And if you want to curl up with a good book and a cup of tea while the rest of your family goes bowling, you say, "Good moms know the value of spending time alone."

Good moms can put their families first by putting themselves first.

Good moms' kids are obedient and well-behaved, but they also misbehave. (They're kids, for goodness' sake.) So the next time your kids misbehave, let your soundtrack be, "My kids aren't perfect. No one's kids are perfect. This is my opportunity to help them make better choices." Good moms don't constantly get raging angry, but they do get mad, and mad isn't bad. So the next time you lose it (and there will be a next time), let your soundtrack be, "I lost it today. Sometimes great moms lose it. I'm still a great mom."

Good moms want to protect their children from pain. But the world is broken, and your kids will get hurt. When it happens, let your soundtrack be, "I'm a good mom even though my child is hurting." And then say, "I'm sorry you're hurting. I'm here with you."

And remember, good moms don't have to do it all, and that's the best soundtrack of all.

Transform instead of Transfer

The truth is that the broken soundtracks that we don't transform into healthy ones get transferred to our children. Sometimes I don't want to do the work of getting my mindset healthier. Staying in my old habits is easier. But my love for my children and my hope that they are as healthy and well-adjusted as possible give me the strength to take care of myself.

My friend Beth grew up hearing from her mom that the best way to keep your marriage happy was to let your husband have things his way. "Don't make waves," her mom would say when her dad got upset. Beth spent the first several years of her marriage miserable and repeating to herself, "Don't make waves."

Love for your children can keep you motivated to be as emotionally healthy as you can be.

But she learned that great marriages have waves, sometimes big waves, and great communication is the best way to ride those waves together. Her new soundtrack became, "Make waves, but don't drown." It was her reminder to approach conflict in a healthy way. She replaced that broken soundtrack and transformed her approach to conflict in a healthy way. In doing so, she passed along a much healthier view of marriage to her own children. It took work (and a lot of counseling), but her mental health and her marriage were better for it.

How to Transform Your Soundtracks

Romans 12:2 says, "Be transformed by the renewal of your mind." What I love about this verse is that it is active. It doesn't tell us to stand there, waiting to be transformed by some miraculous intervention at the hand of God. It tells us exactly how to be changed—by the renewing of our minds. It's saying, *I want you to be transformed, and that begins in your mind, with your thoughts— how you think about me, how you think about you, and how you think about why you were created.*

God gave us the command: Be transformed.

And he told us how to do it: By the renewing of our minds.

When we pay attention to our soundtracks (our thoughts) and replace them with a healthier viewpoint, our mind is renewed and we are transformed. But admittedly, that can be easier said than done. So let me give you some steps to help you do that.

BROKEN SOUNDTRACKS WE DON'T TRANSFORM INTO HEALTHY ONES GET TRANSFERRED TO OUR CHILDREN.

1. Listen to Your Soundtracks

Pay attention to your soundtracks. We are so used to the negative soundtracks we play on repeat, we can be unaware that we are playing them in our thoughts. First, start paying attention to your thoughts and the things you tell yourself. A powerful exercise you can do that will unlock your soundtracks is to use your notes app on your phone or use a journal to document all the things you tell yourself. You'll soon notice patterns in what you say to yourself. What you say may change depending on certain situations, even on how much sleep you had recently.

Then identify which soundtracks are healthy and which are broken.

The most important part of paying attention to your soundtracks is being gentle and loving in the process. You want to be as gentle with yourself as you would with a child working to overcome something difficult. This isn't a time to judge yourself for having the soundtracks; it's time to first become aware and then curious. Practice being a nonjudgmental observer of yourself.

Then ask yourself these three questions:

1. Where did this soundtrack come from?
2. Is there evidence to back it up?
3. Can I transform it with something that builds me up and strengthens my mental health?

2. Look for Evidence

Put your soundtrack on trial. You are the attorney asking questions to find the truth. We all feel like our soundtracks are true because we are so used to them. Why would we question something so familiar it's like breathing, right?

I challenged one of my coaching clients, Jennifer, an attorney and mom of four kids in California, to pay attention to her thoughts. She realized her broken soundtrack was "Nothing ever works out for me." This soundtrack affected her work, her marriage, and of course, her mothering.

Jennifer put her broken soundtrack on trial and looked for evidence to prove her belief that "Nothing ever works out for me." We spent a few sessions talking about her life. I pointed out that she overcame a learning disability and graduated high school with honors, that she built her law firm from the ground up, and that she was brave enough to end an abusive marriage and heal after her first husband betrayed her. She found true love and now has a healthy marriage. Now she is raising four amazing little people. She is killing it.

The evidence showed Jennifer clearly that the soundtrack of "Nothing ever works out for me" was a lie. She had no idea where the broken soundtrack came from (and sometimes that happens), but she knew she needed to replace it with one that was healthy and true.

3. Learn to Replace and Repeat

Once you identify a broken soundtrack, it's time to replace it with one that is true and helpful. And then you repeat it until it becomes your new automatic thought. When building habits that help us thrive, we can't just remove an old habit and leave a vacuum. The same is true with your soundtracks: when you are getting rid of the broken ones, you have to replace them with something. Both nature and my golden retriever abhor a vacuum.

Jennifer replaced "Nothing ever works out for me" with "God is always working things out for me." She looked back on all her successes, struggles, pain, and happiness in life and tracked all the ways God was with her in every moment. She knew that even when life looked the darkest, God was working on her behalf, strengthening her, giving her wisdom, and caring for her.

Jennifer wrote, "God is always working things out for me," on index cards. She placed the cards in her office, on her bathroom mirror, on her window above the kitchen sink, and on her visor in her car. She repeated the new soundtrack to herself until it was second nature.

In her prayer time, she wrote verses that backed up her new soundtrack.

The change in Jennifer's life was so impressive that I took on her new soundtrack too. When I get a new coaching client, I think, "God is always working things out for me." And when I'm

HOW TO REPLACE BROKEN SOUNDTRACKS

① Listen to your soundtacks.

② Look for evidence.

③ Learn to replace and repeat.

hurting and scared because one of my sons is struggling, I say, "Even when I can't see it, God is always working things out for me." The truth is that he is working things out in the big and the little. He never abandons us even if we feel alone for a season.

New healthy soundtracks take time to become part of you. Be sure to put your new soundtracks on repeat until they become second nature.

Sometimes something as simple as a marble jar (or "that stupid marble jar," as it's now known) triggers an unhealthy soundtrack. Sometimes generational trauma saddles us with a toxic soundtrack. Sometimes the messiness of life gives us a soundtrack that is a lie.

It's not your fault you have broken soundtracks. But you have the opportunity and the responsibility to change the soundtracks to ones that are true and kind and that help you be the person and mom God created you to be.

Learning to think about and speak to yourself with love will change how you see yourself and how your kids see you (and themselves) as well.

That is a legacy worth passing on to the next generation.

I Want You to Remember

We don't have to teach our kids everything they need to know by the time they turn eighteen. It's impossible to teach kids everything they need to know before their brains are done developing.

Most of us have soundtracks that play on repeat that we picked up in childhood from adults in our lives. Many of those soundtracks are the ones we heard our moms play to themselves. Generations of women have been burdened with the soundtracks they heard, internalized, and then played themselves.

Broken soundtracks that we don't transform into healthy ones get transferred to our children.

Your love for your children and your hope that they are as healthy and well-adjusted as possible will give you the strength to mother and take care of yourself.

To build healthy soundtracks:

1. Listen to your soundtracks to identify the ones that are healthy or unhealthy.
2. Look for evidence and put your soundtracks on trial.
3. Learn to transform an unhealthy soundtrack with one that is helpful and true. Then repeat it until it becomes an automatic thought.

Journal and Discussion

♥ If you were to sit quietly for a few minutes, what soundtracks would play in your head? What do you notice about the messages you hear?

♥ Think about the condemning or negative soundtracks you hear in your head and speak over your life (and the lives around you). How can you transform those messages into truth?

♥ Do you think generational trauma or legacy burdens are a part of your childhood family? What would it look like to replace those automatic thoughts with kinder ones?

♥ What soundtracks will you play as you transform your thoughts to be more positive and uplifting?

CHAPTER 12

Getting the Love You Need

Neither Mark nor I imagined that after over twenty-five years of marriage, we would end up in a marriage counselor's office. We certainly never imagined we'd be passing a hacky sack back and forth as we took turns sharing our feelings.

Our marriage counselor, a man nearing seventy, smiled as Mark and I tossed that colorful little crocheted ball to each other. He had one wall full of diplomas and another full of books, and I couldn't help but wonder how a man with so much education had come up with such a silly exercise.

It may sound ridiculous, but holding that hacky sack and sharing our unsaid feelings was one of the hardest things we've ever done. And that says a lot because we have been through some stuff together. As a couple, we were great at rolling up our sleeves when life got hard, but baring our souls and being emotionally vulnerable? Nope. We would both want to run away and switch back to discussing the business of the day.

And that's how we ended up in counseling in the first place.

I had shut down. I had put my feelings on the shelf, numb from years of trying to find our sons help for their debilitating migraines. I had finally begun talking to God again. I poured my heart out to him about how I was feeling, and shared with a few girlfriends how I was feeling. The weird thing is that I didn't talk to Mark about my feelings beyond surface-level chitchat. Not only did he not know all the pain I was in, but I also didn't know how he was feeling.

Like a lot of couples, through the years we found ourselves less like romantic partners and more like cochairs of the organization called the family. It felt safer to discuss the day's business than the state of our hearts. We replaced flirty texts with details about school pickups. Romantic time together was replaced (due to exhaustion or illness) with going to bed early.

We were the best at running the organization called the family. We were great at discussing kids and managing home repairs, and balancing schedules with so many kids was an art form we had perfected. But after years of not sharing our hearts, we lacked emotional intimacy. This eventually led to a lack of connection.

We got out of the habit of investing in each other. We had quit talking about what was going on in our hearts. For too long, we were only partners running the family organization.

Learning to reconnect emotionally was messy. The process was sometimes painful. We bumbled around like awkward teenagers on a first date. We needed gentle prodding to help us be comfortable sharing vulnerably with each other again. We needed a counselor with a hacky sack.

My guess is that if you have a spouse, you have been there too. Just as it's easy to sacrifice yourself at the altar of motherhood, it's easy to sacrifice your marriage there too. Sacrificing your marriage's health has consequences far beyond just your marriage. **The marriage relationship is a core part of the family dynamic, and your marriage's health directly affects your mental health.**

But let me take a minute to talk to all the single mamas reading this book. Single motherhood has to be one of the hardest jobs in the world. I don't for one second want to minimize that. And whether you are rocking single motherhood or struggling to get through each day, you have some options here, and I want you to do what your heart needs. Either you can either skip right over this chapter or you can read on. There are some great communication habits here that will translate to how you interact with anyone in your life. If you decide to move on to the next chapter, I support you. But if you choose to hang in, you'll discover some helpful insights into how you communicate with those in your inner circle.

And if you are in a marriage with abuse (physical or emotional), active addiction, or infidelity, or if you feel like you've reached the end of your rope, I want you to put this book down and reach out for help from a professional. When you're ready, this book will still be here, and so will I. But for now, friend, reach out to someone who can help you.

First, let's dive into the not-so-uplifting news. All moms need to be warned that having children can, will, and probably already has temporarily negatively affected your marriage. But don't worry—you're in good company. Mark Johnson, director of the Marriage and Family Studies Laboratory, Binghamton University explains it this way:

> Comparing couples with and without children, researchers found that the decline rate in relationship satisfaction is nearly twice as steep for couples with children than for childless couples. If a pregnancy is unplanned, the parents experience even greater negative impacts on their relationship.
>
> The irony is that even as the marital satisfaction of new parents declines, the likelihood of them divorcing also declines. So, having children may make you miserable, but you'll be miserable together. Worse still, this decrease in

marital satisfaction probably leads to a change in general happiness because the biggest predictor of overall life satisfaction is one's satisfaction with their spouse.[1]

Interestingly, how old your kids are also affects your marital satisfaction. When you're in the throes of infancy and toddlerhood, sleep-deprived and half out of your minds trying to figure out why your baby is crying, your marital satisfaction craters. Then you reach the sweet years of elementary school and your marriage gets a little relief. Unfortunately, that is followed by another marriage stressor when you face the hormones and madness of the teenage years.[2]

Yes, the bad news is that kids will make a marriage different. The shift of focus from being a couple to being parents can make marital satisfaction tank. But there's good news too. **Investing in your marriage will help you overcome the challenges that having kids brings.** That investment will make your marriage stronger and strengthen your own mental health. ("Happy wife, happy life" is so true!)

> Investing in your marriage will help you overcome the challenges that having kids brings. It will make your marriage stronger and strengthen your own mental health.

It's crucial to accept the truth that kids do make life more stressful. Understanding this will help you realize nothing is wrong with you or your marriage—it's comforting to know it's normal. And knowing the facts makes it easier to build healthy habits in your marriage.

Perspective Is Everything

Just as we didn't get a manual on how to invest in our emotional health, we didn't get a manual on how to be an emotionally healthy wife either. Now, some of us got an outdated, legalistic piece of garbage that told us to put our needs and desires on the shelf and to exist only to please our husbands. That is a recipe for depression right there.

We tend to absorb the unspoken rules of marriage from watching our parents' behavior or their attitudes about marriage. And let me go out on a limb here and say that a lot of what we absorbed wasn't helpful.

Some of us grew up in homes where our parents never argued, and we never learned how to handle conflict.

Mary told me her parents never argued in front of her. When she and her husband had their first fight (over whether coffee grounds go in the garbage disposal), she felt certain her marriage would end in divorce.

Maybe you grew up in a home with anger and abuse or emotional roller coasters, and you can't conceive that family life could be any different.

My father died tragically when I was little, and my stepdad was an alcoholic with a brutal temper. When I was growing up, my concept of marriage came from watching my mom walk on eggshells. I watched her wish she could get away, but she felt she lacked the financial ability to support us otherwise.

Or perhaps you grew up in a home with addiction, mental illness, or trauma (death, chronic illness, etc.).

Janine's mom was a diagnosed bipolar schizophrenic. She never knew from day to day whether she'd come home to a mom who was even and calm, manic and out of control, or depressed and sleeping all day. Her dad stayed in the marriage because he felt a duty to his mentally ill wife, but he drank to cope with the stress of it all.

Some homes had a mother doing everything. She worked outside the home, cooked, did housework, helped with

homework—all of it. The father came home from work, kicked back in his recliner, and never gave "pitching in" a second thought.

Leah's mom never took a break. And her dad, whom she adored, didn't do much around the house other than stereotypical things like coach her brother's baseball team. She grew up thinking that's how it should be, and she felt like a failure when she realized she couldn't handle the pressure of doing it all. Instead of communicating her needs, she almost filed for divorce.

It's possible you grew up in a single-parent home and never had the opportunity to see how a married couple handles conflict.

Hannah's mom was an amazing single mom, as most single moms are. She gave her kids everything she could. But the one thing Hannah never saw was how two married people were supposed to interact. It wasn't a life lesson she had access to. Once she married, her mother-in-law was a great resource for her, and so were some of her older friends.

Maybe you grew up in a home where your parents looked perfect to the outside world. But behind closed doors, the relationship was full of contempt, criticism, and pain.

Shannon shared that when her marriage was in crisis, she felt it was her duty to keep their struggles a secret. She never got the help she and her husband needed to make it through those early years of parenting.

For too many of us, the dysfunctional marriage relationship we saw growing up has left us hobbling through life emotionally. At best, we have done what we can with a skewed perspective of what a normal marriage looks like. At worst, we bear the scars of generational abuse or trauma.

Most of us also grew up with romantic comedies telling us

we'd meet Mr. Right and live happily ever after. We would fall perfectly in love, taking life as it comes, hand in hand, until death do us part. But that skewed perspective hasn't helped us either.

In the real world, Mr. Right isn't always right. We aren't always passionately in love. And when life comes at us hard, we hang on for dear life, but we don't always hang on together.

Investing in your marriage is also investing in your happiness. And it's a huge investment in your children's future relationships.

The great news is that we can have healthy marriages no matter what our perspective has been. We can model healthy relationships for our kids. This will help them develop healthier patterns and habits for their own futures.

Habits for a Healthier Marriage

Working toward a healthier marriage can sound overwhelming, but remember that *you don't have to change everything now*. Instead, you can take small steps that will give you big results. As we discovered, your habits and small actions, done repeatedly over time, can change the trajectory of your life.

I'm not saying I'm the expert here, because I'm writing this chapter as Mark and I work on our struggles in counseling. I'm learning these habits along with you, but luckily we can learn from experts together. These aren't habits I've magically come up with; all these habits are ones I'm learning from real experts.

1. Cancel the Criticism

I was shocked to learn that most of what spouses have conflicts over doesn't resolve. Research shows that 69 percent of conflicts are never resolved, even in the happiest marriages.[3]

69% OF MARITAL CONFLICT NEVER GETS RESOLVED, AND THAT'S OK.

The way he leaves his beard trimmings all over the sink.

The way he doesn't like how you kick your shoes off when you walk through the door.

The way he parks the car. (Didn't he see that better parking space?)

He doesn't like to sleep with a fan; you do.

You don't like to eat out; he loves it.

He hates big family events; you think the more the merrier.

Most of our issues don't get fixed. You and your spouse are different people with different personalities. You each have charmingly unique and annoying behaviors. You will probably argue about the same issues when you are twenty-five and seventy-five. We all will. People are people.

The good news is you don't have to fear conflict. The presence of conflict doesn't mean your relationship is doomed to fail. Conflict is simply a sign you live with another person. What really matters is how you handle the conflict. **Conflict handled well leads to conversation, and conversation leads to closeness.**

Conflict-driven conversation typically moves in one of two directions: criticizing (always bad for our relationships) or complaining (surprisingly, not bad for our relationships).

Criticism seems like a normal part of marriage, right up there with negotiating toilet seat placement (please put the lid down) and air temperature in the car (thank you, dual controls).

But according to research, criticism is one of the deadliest habits in marriage and leads to a much higher chance of divorce. Criticism involves attacking someone's personality or character—rather than a specific behavior—usually with blame.[4]

There's a huge difference between criticism that attacks someone and complaints about something someone is doing.

If you tell your husband he's a lazy slob because he always leaves his wet towels on the floor in the bathroom like a jerk, that's criticism. His response will be defensive and probably unkind. On the other hand, if you tell your husband you hate wet towels on the floor because they don't dry well and get moldy and smelly and you would love it if he could hang them back up to dry, *that's* complaining about the wet towel situation. He probably won't feel personally attacked and might be open to discussing the towel situation further.

Criticizing is an atomic bomb for your relationships.

Airing a complaint the right way is beneficial to relationships so that the little annoyances don't fester. According to John Gottman, one of the foremost researchers on marriage, "Expressing anger and disagreement—airing a complaint—though rarely pleasant, makes the marriage stronger in the long run than suppressing the complaint."[5] But criticizing, the attack on someone's personality or character? That is an atomic bomb for your relationship.

Complaining is saying, "I hate that you left dirty dishes all over the counter last night."

Criticizing is saying, "You left all the dirty dishes out on the counter last night because you are thoughtless and have no respect for how we keep the house clean."

Criticizing tends to start with *you*, and complaining tends to start with *I*. It is a small but powerful difference. As author Eric Barker says, "If your sentence starts with 'You always' and doesn't end with 'make me so happy' it's probably a criticism, and you can expect your spouse to respond with both barrels."[6]

Complaining is about the behavior. Criticizing is about the person.

You also shouldn't ignore the damage toxic internal criticism can do. When you mess up and tell yourself the lie that you are dumb or lazy, it's toxic to your own soul.

Becoming aware of how toxic criticism is protects us from accidentally criticizing and hurting our kids too.

Developing a zero-tolerance attitude toward criticism will transform your marriage. Also, you'll become nicer to yourself, and you will improve the relationship you have with your kids.

Changing the criticism habit doesn't happen overnight. It is a long process that starts with simply becoming aware of it, apologizing when it happens (even to ourselves), and giving ourselves grace as we break the bad habit.

Small behaviors, repeated over time, have a big impact.

As you build the habit of allowing healthy complaining and conflict, research shows that when we communicate with our spouse, how we begin any discussion matters. It doesn't just matter, it *really* matters.

A study over six years could predict the likelihood that a couple would divorce by 96 percent based on the first three minutes of a conflict discussion. **When a conversation starts negatively, it's going to stay negative.**

Dr. Gottman suggests the "soft start-up" as a way to go into conversations and to help ensure a positive outcome.

The best soft start-up has four parts:

1. I share some responsibility for this . . .
2. Here's how I feel . . .
3. about a specific situation and . . .
4. here's what I need . . . (positive need, not what you
   don't need).[7]

Here's a real-life example from my good friend Emma. She told me that anytime she has to reprimand her teenagers, her husband "piles on." He turns what would be a quick redirection into a lengthy lecture. I suggested she try Dr. Gottman's method and report back to me. (She's always willing to be my tester for research. Bless you, Emma.) Here's how her actual conversation went using this technique:

Hey babe, can I talk to you about something important?

What's wrong?

(Ha ha, typical response.)

I've been struggling with something lately. I share some responsibility for this because I haven't really taken the time to tell you how I've been feeling. Whenever I get on the girls for something, I've noticed that you jump into the conversation—I'm sure to support me. But for me, it makes me feel like either I am not redirecting them correctly, or that you feel they won't listen to me if you don't back me up. I also feel like it may send the girls a message that they don't really have to listen to me unless you join in. What I need is to be able to redirect the girls, and then if I need some backup, I ask you to support me. Can we try that?

I mean, I guess so. I was only trying to help.

(A little defensive, but he agrees.)

> *I know. And I do appreciate knowing you're*
> *there if I need it. Thank you for being willing*
> *to let me try it on my own, though. It means a*
> *lot to have your support in that way too.*

(I love that Emma didn't "react" to him saying, "I guess so.")

Yep, you got it.

(She did a good job defusing his defensiveness; he responds playfully.)

I love that they both lived out Proverbs 15:1 (NIV), which says, "A gentle answer turns away wrath, but a harsh word stirs up anger." Either of them could have "reacted," but both were gentle with each other, even though they had multiple opportunities to be harsh.

START SOFT

Of course, it's unrealistic to think you're never going to get angry in your marriage. You are. But "anger only has negative effects in a marriage if it is expressed along with criticism or contempt."[8] So building in the habit of canceling criticism with a zero-tolerance policy is key to supporting a healthy marriage.

2. Pile On the Positives

We've learned that we don't have to fear conflict, that many things that annoy us (or our spouse) won't be resolved, and that how we handle conflict is key. But there's another important piece of the puzzle when building healthy habits in our marriages—the frequency of our positive and negative interactions.

According to research, there is a perfect ratio for how many negative versus positive interactions we have with our spouse. In other words, what separates happy couples from miserable couples is the frequency of negative interactions.[9]

For marital stability, a couple needs to have five positive interactions for every negative one. Conflict in your marriage isn't a sign of big trouble. But how we handle that conflict is important. And we need to have more positive interactions than negative interactions to balance things out. When you have a lot more positive interactions than negative ones, conflict isn't as harmful. In other words, pile on the positives.

THE HAPPY MARRIAGE RATIO

5 POSITIVES : 1 NEGATIVE

Goal: 5 positives for every 1 negative interaction

I've used this bit of research to help Mark and me when we are going through hard things. I will intentionally add in extra positives to help balance the negatives. I'm talking simple things—smiling at him across the kitchen, saying something nice to him as we pass in the living room, or buying him his favorite candy.

In his book *The 5 Love Languages*, author Gary Chapman coined the phrase "love tank." He teaches that every person has a love tank that fills when we feel a lot of love from our partner. The downside is that the tank doesn't miraculously stay filled. It has to be refilled every day with positive expressions of love.[10]

The beauty of the love tank is that it gets filled with small expressions of love according to that person's love language. Our love language is the way we feel most loved.

Mark loves gifts, so when I give him something (even a candy bar), he feels my expression of love.

My friend Julie receives love from words of affirmation. When her husband says he's proud of her or thinks she's super smart or a great mom, those remarks fill her tank. He's piling on the positives.

Julie's husband, David, feels love through physical touch—and not just *that kind* of physical touch. He feels loved when she holds his hand while they watch a movie. When she playfully smacks his behind as he walks down the hallway, she's sending him a positive love message. She's piling on the positives.

I'm not saying you have to go around counting the number of positive and negative interactions all the time. But if this is an area where you struggle, *do keep count.*

Knowing the five-to-one ratio can help you to be intentional about piling on the positives and keeping your partner's love tank filled. Then when conflict does arrive, you'll benefit from that positive equity you built up. Your full love tanks and positive equity will ease you through the rough days.

3. Believe the Best

We are biased to see our spouse in one of two ways: positively or negatively. This depends on where we are emotionally, what season of marriage we are in, and the amount of communication we have on average. Let me give some examples:

Your spouse forgets to go by the pharmacy on the way home to pick up your refill when he said he would this morning. You think to yourself,

"Oh, he must have been on autopilot on the way home. He can get it later tonight."

    or

"He is so selfish. Can't he just do something nice for me for once?"

Same trigger (didn't get your refill) but completely different responses. Your response is based on a positive versus negative belief.

Your spouse gets you your favorite box of chocolates for Valentine's Day. You think to yourself,

"I love that he remembered these are my favorite. Even though I'm not eating chocolate right now, I love that he knows what I like."

    or

"I can't believe he bought me chocolate when he knows I'm trying to eat healthy right now!"

Again, same trigger (bought your favorite chocolates) but different responses based on a positive versus negative belief.

Your spouse is late getting home. You think to yourself,

"Traffic must be terrible today. I wonder if he got stuck behind a wreck. I hope he's okay."

    or

"How could he be late and not bother to call me? He doesn't even care about my feelings."

Our core beliefs about someone determine how we view them in light of everyday events.

How we frame our beliefs—positively or negatively—is what determines how we respond in our relationships.[11] Either we

205

believe the best about them, giving them the benefit of the doubt, or we believe the worst. When we believe the best, we assume positive intent.[12] When we believe the worst, we assume negative intent.

Relationships fall into a toxic downward spiral because of a phenomenon called "negative sentiment override." Eric Barker writes about negative sentiment override in *Plays Well with Others*. He tells of a fascinating theory framed by the famous psychologist Albert Ellis, called devilizing. Typically, in healthy relationships, we assume good intentions of those we love. We understand that occasionally people we love make mistakes, but most of the time, their actions toward us are good.

In devilizing, we flip that belief and allow our default to assume negative intent on their part. We go from saying, "You are a great person who sometimes messes up," to saying, "You are the devil in disguise, always out to do me harm." (See where Ellis got the term *devilizing*?) You are no longer biased toward your partner; your bias is against him.

Negative sentiment override doesn't happen overnight; it happens over years. **We assume we know what our spouse is thinking; we see his behavior and filter it through our mood and life experience.** And in a split second, we assume positive or negative sentiment behind everything our spouse does. Once we start down a negative spiral, it's easy to flip to that negative sentiment override.

This is why self-awareness of our automatic reactions and thought patterns is so important.

Developing the habit of assuming positive intent can seem like a subtle change. But as with most habits, the results are massive.

"He can't read my mind" is on a sticky note in my office to remind me that my husband has no idea what I'm thinking or feeling or what I need if I don't tell him.

When I don't tell him what I need, then watch him happily go about his day while I secretly get angry and assume he doesn't care about me anymore? That's a trap I'm not letting myself fall into anymore. My goal is not only to assume positive intent but to reach a state of positive senti-

ment override. I want to reach a place where I see the majority of his behaviors as positive.

Sure, negative things happen, but they are a speed bump, not a sinkhole to fall into. And that knowledge starts with assuming positive intentions.

Proverbs 14:1 (NIV) tells us that "the wise woman builds her house, but with her own hands the foolish one tears hers down." When we are always negative or ready to think the worst and react accordingly, we are like the foolish woman who tears down her house with her own hands.

In day-to-day life, it's easy to start finding fault with those you love. That's why it's in the day-to-day that you have to be intentional about believing the best.

4. Value Vulnerability

All I do is talk. I communicate for a living—I'm writing this book for you, I speak on stages all over the country, I spend my days coaching women in life and business, and I have a weekly podcast where I talk to hundreds of thousands of people. But through the years, other than talking to my husband about the business of running the family organization, I noticed that I felt less and less comfortable talking to him about anything that resembled my feelings. I don't mean talking to him about being mad at him—that I could communicate with no problem. I mean my deeply guarded feelings—my worries, fears, and sorrows.

I first noticed this when we added date nights back into our schedule after several years of abandoning them. After running through current events and surface-level chitchat, I realized I had nothing to talk about.

I casually mentioned this weird pattern to my therapist. She helped me see that at some point growing up, I concluded that being emotionally vulnerable and opening up to a man wasn't safe. At first, I laughed at this idea and reminded her that I was emotionally vulnerable for a living. The world knows how I'm feeling. "Yes," she reminded me, "but the world isn't your husband."

Once again, the truth of the effects of the environment we were raised in came full circle. Even after decades of a happy marriage, something in me didn't feel safe enough to open up with my husband about how I felt and what I needed.

At first, when we threw that hacky sack back and forth, I thought I was shut down as a result of the trauma of not being able to find my sons help for their daily migraine pain. But really I was shut down because I hadn't felt safe enough with Mark to be vulnerable. Not from anything specifically that he had done, but from events in my past.

I questioned why it was easier to be vulnerable with "the world" than with my own husband. My therapist explained that it's because I don't expect the world to meet my needs. I'm not disappointed when I'm vulnerable with the masses and they don't meet my needs. But when I'm vulnerable with my husband and he doesn't meet my needs, I'm devastated.

A healthier way to live is to embrace vulnerability even when it's scary. As the great Brené Brown put it, "I define vulnerability as uncertainty, risk, and emotional exposure. With that definition in mind, let's think about love. Waking up every day and loving someone who may or may not love us back, whose safety we can't ensure, who may stay in our lives or may leave without a moment's notice, who may be loyal to the day they die or betray us tomorrow—that's vulnerability. Love is uncertain. It's incredibly risky. And loving someone leaves us emotionally exposed. Yes, it's scary, and yes, we're open to being hurt, but can you imagine your life without loving or being loved?"[13]

Without some level of emotional vulnerability, I couldn't expect Mark to know what I needed. There was no way he could know how I was feeling. It would be impossible to know how to love me in the way I needed. Feeling like that is a recipe for disappointment, resentment, and quite possibly the worst of all, loneliness in marriage.

After years of feeling like we had a great marriage, Mark and I realized we had not valued vulnerability. We valued our shared faith. We valued being friendly and kind to each other. We valued financial security and our kids getting a good education. We valued our physical health and theirs, and we valued the business of running the family. And while those are all good things, we had not valued being emotionally vulnerable.

Learning to value vulnerability and to get comfortable (or uncomfortable) enough to be vulnerable has been a game changer. It is one of the most intimate and fulfilling things we have done for our marriage.

Motherhood outside of Marriage

Of course, motherhood can exist outside of marriage. Millions of single moms prove that daily. And for those of us who are married, it's important to remember that we are a whole person—our spouse doesn't complete us, and neither do our children. But a great relationship with your spouse is a key factor in your emotional health, and it's a critical component to getting the love you need. Braving the awkwardness of valuing vulnerability, believing the best, piling on the positives, and canceling criticism are all investments in your marriage, yourself, and your children.

A partnership where parents work together to be their best for themselves, each other, and the kids is a gift to everyone. Luckily, we have the tools to build healthy habits into our happily ever after.

I Want You to Remember

Having kids can temporarily negatively affect your marriage. Infancy, toddlerhood, and the teenage years are tough on parents' marital satisfaction. But investing in your marriage will help you overcome the challenges that having kids brings. That investment will make your marriage stronger and strengthen your own mental health.

We tend to absorb the unspoken rules of marriage from watching our parents' behavior or their attitudes about marriage. The good news is that we don't have to repeat what we were exposed to in youth.

Most of what you and your spouse have conflicts over doesn't resolve. Research shows that 69 percent of conflicts are never resolved, even in the happiest marriages. The good news that is you don't have to fear conflict, because the presence of conflict doesn't mean your relationship is doomed to fail. What really matters is how you handle the conflict. Healthy conflict must include a zero-tolerance policy for criticism.

Pile on the positives in your marriage by remembering the five-to-one ratio. You need five positive interactions for every negative interaction. What often separates happy couples from miserable couples is the frequency of negative interactions.

We are biased to see our spouse in one of two ways: positively or negatively. Relationships fall into a toxic downward spiral because of a phenomenon called "negative sentiment override."

Without vulnerability, it is impossible for your spouse to know how to love you in the way you need.

Journal and Discussion

♥ From your perceptions of how marriage *should* be, what kinds of baggage have you carried into your own relationship with your spouse?

♥ We each have a list of the things about our spouse that drive us crazy. Which on the list are you willing to let go?

♥ How does your husband like to be loved? What is his love language?

♥ How do you like to be loved? Make sure to tell your spouse so he can love you like you need to be loved.

♥ How can you pile on the positives to boost your five-to-one ratio?

♥ What is something you've been holding back that you need to be courageously vulnerable about with your spouse?

CHAPTER 13

The Secret Sauce in the Happiness Recipe

When my oldest son was one, we packed up and moved to Memphis. Mark had a new job, and I was excited about a new chapter in our life. It was my first move away from my hometown of Knoxville, and I looked forward to new adventures. My only sadness was from leaving my family and my lifelong friends. It was 1999, and we didn't have social media to keep up with each other easily.

I discovered that finding mom friends was harder than convincing a toddler that zucchini is yummy. Finding new friends was a lot like dating. It felt like a long series of putting myself out there and seeing if I was a good fit with another person.

Like with dating, I was always trying to figure things out:

She looks nice; I wonder if she wants another friend.
She seems great, but her kids are bonkers. Pass.

She seems unapproachable, but maybe she's just exhausted
  and would love a new friend!

She has kids who are waaay too well-behaved. Will she judge
  my wild heathens?

My first two Memphis friends were Rachel and Emily. Rachel
and I met at a Chick-fil-A playland, a perfect friend pick-up spot
for moms of young kids. Emily and I met at the Memphis Zoo by
the gorilla exhibit.

There is a flow to talking to a potential friend. I start by commenting on their kids. If that goes well, I make a little small talk.
If the small talk goes well, I introduce myself. If no weird vibes
pop up, I follow up with, "Let's get the kids together to play at the
park sometime. Let them burn off some energy." This is mom
code for *I want to be your friend.*

Rachel and I became great friends. She took us to her church.
We spent at least two days a week camped out at each other's
houses while our kids played. We even tackled organizing projects together. I always felt better after seeing Rachel. She was a
good friend—supportive, kind, and honest. And I always felt like
I could let my guard down and be real when I was with her.

I even told Rachel I wanted to figure out a way to help people
on the internet one day. I must have sounded crazy. I had no idea
what helping people looked like, and in 1999 selling stuff on eBay
was the only way to make money on the internet. There was only
painfully slow dial-up, and Google had just launched. There was
no foreseeable way to build a business helping people online back
then. But Rachel listened to my crazy ideas, offered feedback, and
said, "If anyone can figure that out, it might as well be you!"

Emily, on the other hand, was a different story. We did the
normal things—playdates, trips to each other's houses, etc., but
our relationship wasn't the same as my relationship with Rachel.

FRIENDSHIP FLAGS

GREEN FLAGS

◀ They respect your
boundaries

◀ You can be
yourself around
them

◀ They are happy
when you succeed

◀ You feel better
after you spend
time with them

◀ They accept you
for who you are

RED FLAGS

◀ They often
criticize you

◀ They are dismissive
about your dreams
and achievements

◀ They always have
something negative
or gossipy to say

◀ They always
"one-up" you

◀ They ask for
favors but don't
return them

Though Rachel teased me about my embrace of the "messy aesthetic" that I styled my home with, she wasn't hurtful to me. She was there for me and encouraged me. Emily's teasing, though, always left me feeling bad about myself. And when she could see my feelings were hurt, she'd say, "Oh, Alli. I was just kidding." After a few months, I realized that, more often than not, I felt worse about myself and my life when I hung around Emily.

Looking back, I didn't see the red flags from Emily.

- During our first meeting, she put down a friend of hers in a story she told me.
- She constantly criticized how I did things.
- I was secretly relieved when our plans fell through.
- I felt exhausted and sad after I saw her.

I confided to Emily that I was on a supertight budget. I had $100 per week for the family's food, diapers, gas, and any extras that always came up. She often invited us to do activities that were way more than what I could afford. Her invitations were not the problem. Her commentary was.

After inviting me to a pricey event, she would say, "I know you probably can't afford it, but I didn't want you to feel left out." She followed up with an insulting, "If you ever need any tips on managing your budget, I'm great at it! Just let me know." Although her voice sounded sweet, her words were condescending and embarrassed me.

Once, at a social gathering, she told the women we were standing with, "It's such a shame that Alli isn't going to be able to go with us on our beach weekend. I've offered to help her manage her budget, but she hasn't taken me up on it yet. Maybe next summer, right, Alli?" My face went hot, and I wanted to cry and run out the door.

I loved her kids, my kids loved her kids, and I did like her, but over time it became clear that I had to break away from her. I had to end the friendship for my emotional health. Now, I feel about confrontation the way I feel about cantaloupe—I don't want anything to do with it. Even the smell of confrontation (or cantaloupe) makes me feel queasy.

Over the next few weeks, I lied and faked two vague kid illnesses. (You can't get away with this because of social media now. It keeps us honest.) I became too busy to meet up and tried to slowly slink away from this nightmare frenemy.

Emily was not having it, and she showed up at my house on a Saturday afternoon to talk about why I was avoiding her. I planned to let the friendship fade, but she wasn't a let-it-fade kind of girl. She may have been a bad friend, but she was more mature than I was (back then) and wanted to talk it out. I was trapped and getting nauseous (worse than being forced to eat a bowl of cantaloupe!), and I broke down and cried and explained that I didn't think we could be friends anymore.

I won't say it ended well. She told me I was overly sensitive, and she couldn't help it if I wasn't able to handle a little good-natured kidding. Her parting words were, "No hard feelings, Alli. I hope you find the friend you are looking for."

Somehow, I felt wrong for telling her the truth. I may have felt like I was being a jerk because of the belief that women are always supposed to be "nice." Or I may have felt that way because I'd heard the "seventy times seven" sermon on forgiveness more than I could count.

Should I have turned the other cheek and continued in what was obviously an unhealthy relationship? Was I showing the kind of love that God wanted me to show Emily by telling her I didn't think we could be friends? A soundtrack played on repeat in my mind: "Love is patient, love is kind. It does not envy, it does not boast. . . . It keeps no record of wrongs."[1]

I had been patient and kind, and I certainly hadn't boasted about anything—quite the opposite. I shrank into a tiny little version of myself anytime Emily and I were together. Did God intend for me to be friends with someone who left me feeling shamed, drained, and discouraged after every encounter? Surely that couldn't be right either.

I wish I had the understanding about toxic relationships back then that I have now. I interviewed Gary Thomas on my podcast about his book *When to Walk Away: Finding Freedom from Toxic People*. He taught me that we have to have boundaries to protect ourselves from those who hurt us repeatedly. Gary taught me that if someone is trying to get you to stop being yourself or doing what you believe God wants you to do, that person is toxic *for you*. It's an attack on your being and an attack on your mission.

If someone is trying to get you to stop being yourself or doing what you believe God wants you to do, that person is toxic *for you*. It's an attack on your being and an attack on your mission.

I felt like my mission in that season of life was to be the best wife to my husband and the best mom for my kids. Being close to someone who drained me emotionally left me frazzled and more easily frustrated with my kids.

Not only was Emily hurting me, by default, but she was also hurting my kids. The word *toxic* is weighty; I get it. It's not a word we should throw around lightly. I'm not saying Emily was toxic; I'm saying she was toxic *for me*.

Gary went on to say, "Humility calls us to realize that what is toxic for us may not be toxic for others. If you have a toxic experience with someone that leaves you frustrated and discouraged, rethinking conversations late at night, finding your blood pressure rising, and (especially this) seeing it keep you from being present with loved ones long after the toxic interaction is over, then for you that relationship isn't healthy."[2]

To be emotionally healthy for my kids, I had to end my relationship with Emily. I continued to invest in relationships that helped me be the woman and mom I wanted to be and felt called to be.

The Power of Friendship

Fast-forward twenty-four years and my life looks much different. Four more boys arrived in our family. My days of being a stay-at-home mom changed too. Now I run a company that helps people thrive all over the world through the internet. Isn't it crazy how we sometimes get little ideas and have dreams that seem impossible? But over time, when we keep taking little steps (remember the power of 1 percent better), we can reach our dreams. Unfortunately, as my company and my family grew, my friendships took a back seat to my family and my work.

Author Eric Barker told me on my podcast that the thirties are where our friendships go to die.[3] I don't disagree. Work, kids, marriage, the never-ending laundry—it's easy to let friendships slide. But friendships make us happier than any other kind of relationship.

How can that be? All the joy that kids bring? The deep affection we feel for our spouse? *Friends make us happier?* Scientists have been tracking this happiness factor with hundreds of thousands of people, and it's true.[4]

We choose our friends based on how we feel about them: Do they "get" us, do we feel known and understood,

Friendships are the happiest of relationships.

do we click? We aren't necessarily bound to our friends like we are in family relations or job requirements; we just like them. And because of that, friendships are special. We don't squabble with them over the division of labor or whose turn it is to put the whining four-year-old back to bed. Friend time is fun time.

The beauty of a healthy friendship is it reminds us that we are whole people outside our role as moms. A good, healthy friendship encourages us on bad days, strengthens us on weak days, and gives us a good kick in the pants when we need that too. The power of friendship is that it provides the rich community we need in every season of our lives. And we especially need it in every season of motherhood.

Our children make life meaningful, but friends make life happier.

Mom friendships benefit our kids. We've seen over and over that investing in our emotional health helps our children grow to be better adjusted, have healthier relationships, and be more successful in life. The great news is that having healthy friendships helps our children's cognitive development.[5]

Researchers spent time with over one thousand moms and were struck by the fact that the larger the social network a mom had (averaging three to four friends), the better her children did developmentally at age two.[6]

Investing in healthy friendships is also an investment in yourself and your family.

It makes sense that a woman who has a support system outside of her family is likely to have more emotional support. When life gets hard or a crisis happens, she has people to help her.

The study's coauthor shared,

Outside the family context, mothers with larger social networks may be able to draw on resources from those networks that alleviate some of the burdens associated with parenting. This may include emotional support, tangible support in the form of babysitting or help with errands, and the transfer of knowledge around high-quality daycare or other childhood programs. These resources may reduce parenting stress and improve maternal mental health, both of which are positively associated with child cognitive development.[7]

One of these great resources to help mothers create a bigger network is social media. One of my favorite parts about it is how it connects our support systems. When the boys were little and Mark and I moved every few years for his career, social media didn't exist. We made friends by bravely going to new and unfamiliar places and talking to random strangers. But now when people move, their networks can be interconnected.

YOUR FRIENDSHIPS BENEFIT YOUR WHOLE FAMILY.

When my childhood friend Carly moved from Atlanta to Dallas, one of her Atlanta friends was quick to introduce her to her Dallas friends via Facebook and Instagram. When Carly moved, the Dallas people felt familiar because they had a common bond with her Atlanta friend. Carly said, "I was expecting to feel isolated and lonely when we moved, but my friend in Atlanta made sure that didn't happen. It's like I had a ready-made network of friends."

The Loneliness Epidemic

We know the importance of healthy friendships for a healthy mindset: having friends is great for us and our kids too. But for many moms, motherhood is a lonely experience.

For new moms, the insecurity that comes with being a mom for the first time can be isolating. We don't want to seem like we don't know what we're doing, yet in reality, we have no clue. So we muddle through, often trying to figure things out ourselves.

For moms coming from a full-time work experience, maternity leave can be both a blessing and a time of surprising loneliness. Going from days filled with adult conversation to days filled with crying and spit-up is rough. It's like being magically promoted to the Queen of England, but the day-to-day time is spent emptying garbage cans and plunging clogged palace toilets. **Being a mother is the most wonderful gift, but the day-to-day can be a real drag.**

Different seasons of motherhood can also contribute to this loneliness. As I mentioned earlier, Mark and I moved a lot. During the first ten years of our marriage, we moved six times for his career—not just moved houses but moved cities and states. All five boys were born in different cities. After the fourth move, I gave up on trying to make friends. Going through the awkward phase of trying to get to know people and develop friendships only to move again was too much.

I was with my kids all the time, and my husband was home in the evenings and on the weekends. But I was still so lonely. I needed girlfriends.

I began to build intentional community with women online from all over the world. Some of my closest friends today are ones I met on Twitter fifteen years ago. The technology may change (no more tweeting—now we FaceTime and plan girls' weekends) as the years go by, but the friendships keep growing. Social media has been a lifeline in building my company and building my friendships. But when it comes to loneliness, we have to be smart about how we use social media so it is a blessing and not a curse.

Loneliness is an epidemic. More than three in five people say they are lonely. From 2018 to 2020, loneliness grew by 13 percent.[8] Loneliness is linked to anxiety and depression.[9] Loneliness and poor relationships are linked to a 29 percent increased risk of heart disease and 32 percent increased risk of stroke.[10] And here's a maybe not-so-surprising statistic: heavy social media use and loneliness go hand in hand. Seventy-three percent of heavy social media users reported feeling lonely as opposed to 52 percent of light users.[11]

Social media can be such a valuable tool for helping us feel connected, but it also has the capacity to make us feel lonelier if we don't use it intentionally to build connections.

Active social media use makes us feel good. Active use is when you comment on your friends' posts or send a meme to make a friend laugh. You'll feel connected and happier when you use social media intentionally to build and deepen friendships.

But passive scrolling makes us feel worse. Passive scrolling doesn't connect us with others. When we aren't connecting with people, a part of our brain can't help but compare our real life with other people's best moments. Real life is full of kid tantrums, misbehaving dogs, and arguments with others.[12]

ACTIVE SOCIAL MEDIA	PASSIVE SOCIAL MEDIA
• Commenting on friends' posts	• No commenting
• Connecting with others	• Endless scrolling
• Makes you feel better	• Makes you feel worse

Loneliness doesn't mean you are alone. Being lonely can happen in crowds, with your family, and even around a group of friends. I've felt lonely in a crowd more often than I'd like to remember, and my guess is you have too. Loneliness isn't about being around people or not. **Loneliness depends on how meaningful our relationships are.**

We know how important good friendships are, how widespread loneliness is, and how damaging loneliness can be to our emotional and physical health. Now let's identify some easy-to-do habits to help build the community, support system, and relationships we need.

Habits for Healthy Friendships

1. Make Peace with Friend Dating

As with dating, you always look for chemistry with a potential friend. You have to meet people, make small talk, and then subtly figure out if they want to hang out again. Sure, it's awkward, but you have to make peace with the process. Need healthier friends? Go find them. My favorite spots are church groups and school gatherings. From preschool all the way to high school—your kid's friend's mom could be a potential new best friend.

Could you get hurt? *It happens.*

Will you meet a lot of people you don't click with? *Yup.*

Women with such widely different beliefs and parenting styles that you don't think you want to get invested? *Of course.*

Women who will brush you off because you don't fit their mental picture of a friend? *Sadly, yes. If only they knew how lovely you are!*

My friend Laura even met a great friend by using an app to find friends. It's owned by (as weird as this sounds) a dating app.

However you find a new friend, it's worth the small talk when you find someone who gets you. The kind of friend who arrives at your house when it's messy and doesn't even notice. She even tells you how amazing you look a week after having a baby, even though you catch a glimpse in the mirror and see the milk stains on your T-shirt, your hair probably has two scrunchies lost in it, and you haven't showered since the baby arrived.

2. Bundle Friend Time with Everyday Activities

Friendship is voluntary. We are friends with others because we *want* to be friends. There aren't natural systems that hold friends together like there are in families. As a result, we have to fit time for friends into our already full days.

When I was working as a stay-at-home mom, I had time to see my other mom friends during the day. We met on trips to the zoo, at playgrounds, and sitting on each other's couches, trying to get some peace while our kids watched a movie. But when I started building my first business online, a good bit of the time I had spent with friends shifted to time spent on my business. And now that I run my coaching business, there's even less time. To fit in friend time, I began bundling friend time with "normal life." Bundling friend time with my everyday activities helps me stay in touch with my friends.

My friend Laura and her new bestie whom she met on the friend app both work full-time. They don't have time for long phone calls to catch up, so once a week they FaceTime while they make dinner. That way they can see each other as they chop veggies and prepare meals. It's their Tuesday evening tradition.

Bundle friend time with everyday activities to keep connected.

I'm an entrepreneur at heart, and I love starting new projects and businesses. Anytime I can create something that will help women thrive, I'm in. I've even bundled my friend time with work by inviting a friend to start a business with me.

I started Called Creatives with my friend Lisa. Called Creatives is a coaching and training community for women who feel called to write and speak. We help women step into their calling, give them friendship in a community of like-minded women, and provide them training to be successful as speakers and authors. Lisa and I had been good friends for years. We were both authors and

BUNDLE FRIEND TIME.

speakers with a passion for helping other women answer and live out their unique calling. Running the business together keeps us connected. We talk business and share what's on our hearts many times a week. We even have company-planning weekends at Disney to bundle even more fun friend time in our business. Why not plan the next quarter of the business while standing in line for the Tower of Terror? Work + Friends + Fun = the best bundle.

No matter what you bundle—work, laundry, dinner—schedule time with friends. With so many responsibilities, you've probably found it's too easy to let friendships fall through the cracks. You don't always need to get away on girls' weekends or for long lunches (though that would be lovely, and you should do it if you can); you can include your friends in everyday life. **When you bundle your everyday activities with friend time, you can make the boring parts of life meaningful and even fun.**

3. Honor Your Priorities

There's a chemistry between good friends that defies explanation sometimes. My friend Sarah and I are polar opposite about faith, politics, and most parts of our parenting styles. We love each other and have the best time together only because years ago we decided to stop trying to convert each other to our way of thinking. The run-up to the presidential election every four years is interesting for us both. We always passionately root for opposite candidates. We flat out agreed not to talk about it to each other. It's how we stay sane.

When our kids were little, we would occasionally laugh or roll our eyes at the other's rules that we didn't agree with. Our three oldest children are the same age, but then I went and had two more younger kids. Our differing parenting styles were most obvious and most annoying when all the kids were together and wanted to watch a movie or TV show. What was entertaining for the older kids wasn't always age appropriate for the little kids. My rule was that when all the kids were together, we would watch something safe for everyone. You can imagine the exasperation from Sarah and eye rolls from our older kids.

I stuck to my values and invited Sarah and the older kids to express how frustrated they were. I reminded them we could all watch what we wanted in our own homes. We agreed that when we were all together, we would err on the side of caution with our movie choices.

Sarah and I are long past parenting-choice squabbles. We love and respect each other. We may have opposite beliefs about things like faith and politics, but we don't let that affect our friendship.

My priority in friendship is not that my friends need to have the same beliefs about everything as I do. Would it be easier if we did? Of course, but there's a great benefit in learning from others and understanding other points of view. My priority in friendship is that I have a friend with a positive outlook. A friend who is emotionally healthy with a healthy mindset. One who is trustworthy and smart and has a can-do attitude. I've noticed in the past ten years or so, I also gravitate toward friends who are writers or entrepreneurs. We understand each other's experiences. We have lived through the good times and stressful times that go along with charting a unique path in life.

Everyone has different priorities in friendships.

Some may prioritize friendships with those who share their faith.

Some may prioritize friendships with those who have same-aged kids.

Some may prioritize friendships with those who fit naturally into their everyday life.

Some may prioritize friendships with those who like to go and do.

Some may prioritize friendships with those who like to run or read or drink coffee.

My cousin Leanne prioritizes friendships with those with whom she shares many common interests. She looks for people who share her political beliefs, who love the outdoors, and who love mountain biking.

Knowing what you do and don't like in friendships helps you know where to put your time and energy.

After identifying your priorities in friendships, you'll want to honor those priorities by identifying your boundaries. As relationship expert Nedra Glover Tawwab says, "Boundaries are expectations and needs that help you feel safe and comfortable in your relationships. Expectations in relationships help you stay mentally and emotionally well."[13]

WHEN IT COMES TO BOUNDARIES FOR ME

☑ I will not let a friend use guilt to have more of my time or energy than I have to give.

☑ I refuse to spend my time with a friend who wants to gossip for the majority of our time together.

☑ I will not intentionally spend time with people who hurt me or my family members. This is especially true if they disguise it as a joke or try to deny it.

☑ I refuse to get pressured into activities or obligations that I don't want to do.

☑ I will not spend time with friends who have an overwhelmingly bitter or negative mindset or victim mentality.

Through the years, I've developed some boundaries that help me feel safe and comfortable in my friendships:

- I will not let a friend use guilt to have more of my time or energy than I have to give.
- I refuse to spend time with someone who wants to gossip for the majority of our time together.
- I will not intentionally spend time with people who hurt me or my family members. This is especially true if they disguise it as a joke or try to deny it.
- I refuse to be pressured into activities or obligations that I don't want to do.
- I will not spend time with someone who has an overwhelmingly bitter or negative mindset or a victim mentality.

Your Friends = Your Future

Who we spend our time with is who we will become. If we spend our time around people who are negative, we will develop a more negative mindset. If we spend our time with people who invest in themselves and work to be as emotionally healthy as they can be, that will rub off on us as well. Healthy, loving friendships are a gift from God. They are a key part of a happier life and a healthier mindset.

Friendships that are flexible, fun, and fulfilling are one of the best gifts you can give to yourself and your children. Our friends make us stronger, better, and more loving. They help us conquer the challenges of motherhood. Healthy friendships are the secret sauce in the happiness recipe of life, so build habits that grow and support those friendships.

I Want You to Remember

If someone is trying to get you to stop being yourself or doing what you believe God wants you to do, that person is toxic *for you*. It's an attack on your being and an attack on your mission.

Friendships are the relationships that make us happiest. We develop friendships because we genuinely like each other. Deep friendships make us happy and benefit our whole families. Community brings support for mothers, which is especially important during difficult seasons of life.

Loneliness is based on how meaningful your relationships are. Mothers can be at risk of feeling lonely. A lot of passive social media use causes an increase in depression and loneliness.

To fit friend time into a busy life, you can bundle friend time with "normal life." Bundling friend time with your everyday activities can help you stay in touch with your friends. It can make the boring parts of life meaningful and even fun.

In friendship, honor your priorities and protect your boundaries. Knowing what you do and don't like in friendships helps you know where to put your time and energy. Protecting your boundaries allows you to feel safe and comfortable in your friendships.

Journal and Discussion

♥ What is the state of your friendship landscape right now? Is it good and healthy? Nonexistent or sparse? What changes might you need to make to get or keep things in good shape?

♥ Which friendships do you need to prioritize right now? What are you doing to make sure they receive the care and nurturing they require?

♥ When you take an objective look at your friendships, which are the toxic (for you) ones that will require some evaluation or confrontation before you allow those friends to continue in close community with you?

♥ What is one way you can start bundling friend time?

CHAPTER 14

The Secret Art of Confident Motherhood

Our oldest son, Justin, graduated college recently, even though it seems like just yesterday that I was worried about him refusing to try vegetables. The days were slow, while the years flew by. The morning of graduation, Justin asked if one of his friends could sit next to me at lunch after the ceremony. He said, "His mom isn't super easy to talk to like you, and he needs some life advice. He's always heard me talk about how great you are with stuff like that."

The thought that he told his college friends how great I am was about the best gift I could receive as a mom.

At twenty-four, Justin is his own man, with a job and adult worries and stressors. I no longer actively parent him, but I will always be his mom. I will always be someone he can come to for understanding and advice. *Once a mom, always a mom.* That never changes.

I could give you an extensive list of all the mistakes I made with that boy. I could shock you with stories of my failures, his poor decisions, and situations I screwed up. Raising your babies to adulthood is messy, but thank God we have to get it right only half the time. With our 50 percent and God's 100 percent, our kids can turn out amazing.

Remember how I told you at the beginning of this journey that this is not a parenting book but a book about motherhood? Parenthood is all about how to raise your kids to behave in polite society and even how to make them mind without losing yours. It's about structure, discipline, guidance, and conformity to social and cultural norms.

Motherhood is about intimacy. It's about knowing ourselves and our children at the deepest level and loving unconditionally from that place.

According to psychotherapist Naomi Stadlen, author of *How Mothers Love*, "Intimacy is crucial for a person to realize his or her potential to the maximum. It enables a person to reach genuine original, loving and creative energy. . . . This doesn't mean mothers have to be perfect creatures—they just need to recognize their power."[1]

Motherhood invites us to know and love ourselves unconditionally.

The idea of loving our children unconditionally doesn't need a book. There is no love like a mother's love for her children. **But motherhood also invites us to know and love ourselves unconditionally.** Motherhood can teach us about ourselves and allow us to transform ourselves for the better. And knowing and loving ourselves is not as easy to do. To remain you while raising them, you have to stay connected to who you are and learn and grow throughout your motherhood journey.

Easier said than done, right? There isn't a magic recipe for mothering or parenting. But it's not like we are flying blind either. We can learn from women who are a few steps ahead. In this age of information, we are blessed with wisdom from data from thousands of studies. We can also rely on our faith, our values, and most importantly, our instincts about our own children.

You know the expression "Mother knows best"? For you, it's true! The choices you make for yourself and your family are right *for you*. They may not be the right choices for others—we all have different personalities, superpowers, budgets, kids' needs, and family dynamics.

But you have permission to make decisions based on what's right for you, what you need (thank you, magic question), and what is important to your family. No more comparison, no more shame, no more guilt. Let's say goodbye to all that craziness.

Permission to Say Goodbye to Mom Guilt

You know modern motherhood is broken with all the impossible standards, expectations, and mom guilt that have been heaped on us. But you've been given permission to say goodbye to the mom guilt that has been beating you up.

You have broken down the myths that tried to tell you what "good moms" look like.

You know the truth that being a good mom doesn't mean you sacrifice yourself on the altar of martyred mothers. That doesn't help anyone. Your kids need you to be emotionally healthy.

You understand that good moms' kids are sometimes wild rule-breaking heathens. I know mine have been. They will make choices that leave you dumbfounded, shaking your head in exasperation. But that's all a part of raising kids.

You learned that good moms do get angry, and with good reason. Mad isn't bad, but learning to understand, manage, and process anger in a healthy way is possible.

You see that good moms can't always protect their children from pain, nor should they. What good moms can do is help their children feel loved and give them tools to cope when pain touches their lives.

You are relieved to know that good moms not only don't have to be Wonder Woman, but if you were, it would mess up your kids.

Mom guilt makes you lie to yourself, and the only way to fight a lie is with the truth. **You kill mom guilt by fighting back with truth, evidence, and facts.** When you take a night away and grab dinner with a girlfriend, mom guilt might say, "I'm not doing enough; I'm being selfish." You can fight back with the truth that friendships are good for your emotional health and your happiness.

It's easy to let a shouldstorm overwhelm you with all the thoughts that you *should* be cooking for the kids and *should* be cleaning the house. But when you zoom out and think about it, it's clear that one night of not picking up the house and the kids eating take-out pizza is not a big deal. The kids need a happy mom more than they need a tidy living room and a home-cooked meal that night.

When mom guilt creeps in and says, "Your daughter lied about eating her veggies and threw them away. You aren't raising her well," you can fight back with the truth that when bad choices happen, you address them, but you focus on the general trajectory of your child's life. When she is doing everything else right but decides to lie about broccoli, it doesn't mean she's headed for a life of crime. Instead, it gives you a teachable moment to help her

THE MAGIC OF MOTHERHOOD IS IN WHO YOU ARE, NOT JUST WHAT YOU DO.

know you love her whether she loves veggies or not. (And also, to help her understand the importance of telling the truth.)

When mom guilt pops up, I want you to ask yourself, "Would God say this to me?" I know he wants you to be emotionally, physically, and spiritually healthy for you and your family. He's not going to tell you that you are not enough. He's not going to tell you that you are not doing enough. And he'll remind you that just as you (as his child) sometimes mess things up, your kids will too. But that doesn't mean God is doing a terrible job as your Father or that you are a bad mom.

When you feel the weight of mom guilt on your shoulders, remember this truth most of all—God chose you to be a mom. And mom guilt doesn't come from him.

The Best Investment

Do you want to know the secret art of confident motherhood? It's you. The best investment you can make in motherhood is in yourself: building your emotional health and forming small helpful habits that improve your life.

Mothering is a gift that unwraps itself in each new season. It invites you to mother not only your children but yourself as well. As you learn to care for yourself and invest in what helps you thrive, you are able to remain you while raising them.

Your emotional health is made up of your mental, spiritual, and relational health. How you care for yourself matters. It impacts your daughters and your sons. It encourages your daughters to remember they are worth it. Their emotional health is key to their own motherhood journey. And it impacts your sons by giving them healthy, realistic expectations of the women in their future.

The more you invest in yourself and the more emotionally healthy you are, the more your kids will stay close to you

as they mature. You won't lose them when they turn eighteen like that stupid marble jar implied. The more emotionally healthy you are, the more that you will be the one they continue to come to for advice and encouragement in adulthood.

You'll never stop being their mom, and the transition from parent to friend is pretty awesome too.

A Visit to My House

When I think about my most treasured experiences in the sisterhood of motherhood, I think of the times I have spent with other moms in each other's homes. If you came to my house, we'd sit at my dining room table, you with your coffee and I with my green tea.

A VISIT TO MY HOUSE

We could sit on the off-white couch I finally bought after two decades of varying shades of brown couches to hide all the dirt. But no one eats or drinks within a five-foot radius of the white couch. Not even me. I would apologize for the golden retriever hair on the table but wouldn't bother jumping up and wiping it down because we're good enough friends. And I don't need to pretend I'm tidier than I am.

You might tell me that you feel guilty for letting your buttons get pushed and yelling at the kids. And you can't believe how hard parenting is. Or you might admit that you worry they will grow up and you won't have a good relationship and you'll lose them. Or maybe you'll share that you have overwhelming guilt that you aren't a good enough mom. And then you might tell me you obsess about getting it wrong.

I would nod and tell you that I've felt all those things many times. You are not alone in your feelings, and every mom struggles with each one at some point. I would admit to you that for a season I was the mom who poured from an empty cup that left me feeling bitter, ready to snap, and alone.

I don't want you to beat yourself up for being human. I want you to have all the wisdom and tools that it took me decades to develop. I would love hearing how you are investing in your emotional health.

I'd want to hear that you are protecting yourself by unfollowing the accounts that trigger mom guilt and muting the ones you can't unfollow because you don't want to have to explain it when you see them at your kid's school.

I'd want to know that you are breaking the hold of generational trauma in your family by not allowing that behavior or belief to continue, making the decision that the unhealthy thought patterns and coping strategies will not continue to the next generation.

If you're going through a difficult season, I want you to learn to care for yourself in new ways, asking for help from those in your circle and learning to treat yourself with more kindness and care than you knew you could.

And, like most moms, at some point you might tell me you feel like you've lost yourself in your role as a mom. We would pause at this moment of vulnerability, looking out the window because if we looked into each other's eyes, we might both lose it and cry.

After we finished our coffee and tea, we would go out to the back porch and sit. As we watched the evening unfold, the fireflies would light up the backyard and give us a show.

We would marvel at how mothering has brought a joy otherwise unknown to us this side of heaven. That sweet child is our heart plucked from our very chest. We would look at each other across the porch and nod when we tried to come up with words to describe how much we love our children. But we'd come up short. Words don't do this deep, life-changing, all-encompassing love justice.

As our visit wrapped up, I would give you a last hug and remind you of the truth you need to hear: **Investing in yourself and your emotional health is the secret art of confident motherhood.**

You are a great mom. How do I know? I know because we've spent time together crushing the myths that have had us locked in mom guilt for far too long.

Investing in yourself and your emotional health is the secret art of confident motherhood.

Modern motherhood may be broken, but you are breaking free and embracing these truths:

Great moms make mistakes.
Great moms lose their tempers.
Great moms need a break.
Great moms are exhausted.
Great moms invest in themselves.
Great moms are always learning.
Great moms are always growing.
Great moms learn that emotional health is the greatest gift they can give their kids.

INVESTING IN YOURSELF AND YOUR EMOTIONAL HEALTH IS THE SECRET ART OF CONFIDENT MOTHERHOOD.

As you move forward on your motherhood journey, not only can you break free from the good-mom myths, but you can also embrace these truths. Write them on your bathroom mirror. Put them on a sticky note in your car. Let them be constant reminders that you are a great mom. Remember:

You are on the right track.
You are arming yourself with wisdom.
You have a unique superpower.
You were chosen by God to be a mother.
You are discovering how to honor your needs.
You are learning new confidence in your motherhood.
And you are investing in yourself.
You are a great mom.
Well done.

I Want You to Remember

Mom guilt makes you lie to yourself, and the only way to fight a lie is with the truth. You kill mom guilt by fighting back with truth, evidence, and facts. God chose you to be a mom, and mom guilt doesn't come from him.

The best investment you can make in motherhood is in yourself: building your emotional health and forming small habits that improve your life. Your emotional health is made up of your mental, spiritual, and relational health. How you care for yourself matters. It impacts your daughters and your sons. It encourages your daughters to remember they are worth it. Their emotional health is key to their own motherhood journey. And it impacts your sons by giving them healthy, realistic expectations of the women in their future.

Investing in yourself and your emotional health is the secret art of confident motherhood. Great moms make mistakes. Great moms lose their tempers. Great moms need a break. Great moms are exhausted. Great moms invest in themselves. Great moms are always learning. Great moms are always growing. Great moms learn that emotional health is the greatest gift they can give their kids.

Journal and Discussion

♥ What have you learned about yourself through the course of this book? Write those things down so you don't forget them.

♥ Which of the myths are you most excited to leave behind?

♥ Which myth will be the toughest for you to bust on a day-to-day basis?

♥ In what ways are you committed to investing in yourself to ensure you are at your best for your family?

Acknowledgments

Remaining You While Raising Them has been a joy to bring to the world because of the encouragement, wisdom, and partnership of many wonderful people. It takes a village to raise a child and to write a book. I'm blessed with a great village!

First and Foremost, My Family

Mark—What a journey these past few years have been. Through it all, I've never felt more loved and known. Who knew being vulnerable would be so fun? I love you forever. Thank you for always being my biggest encourager.

Kids—You are the joy of my life. Words can't do this love justice, and I hope my actions show you every single day how much I adore you all. It is the great honor and thrill of my life to be your mother. I would fight a bear blindfolded with a butter knife for every one of you.

My mom, my mother-in-law, and my grandmother—Thanks for giving me such great examples of confident motherhood. I love you!

The *RYWRT* Brain Trust

Thank you, Carol Jones, for your wisdom and your amazing ability to help me clarify my thoughts. Ashley Collins, PhD, thank you for being my lead researcher and giving all the research double and triple checks. Heather Ablondi, you bring such leadership as well as insight to this message. Thank you! Thank you to Jenna Burns and Lisa Whittle for always having my back. Melody Belotte, thank you for always being two steps ahead of me. Big love to Danielle LaGree, Jordan Petty, Ashley Haupert, Rachel Sinclair, Colleen Smith, and Jenny Ingram, who read early drafts and lovingly told me what they loved and what I needed to clean up.

Lysa TerKeurst and team, thank you for helping to ideate, structure, and make sense of all the ideas swirling in my mind. The time we shared planning and dreaming about this message was invaluable.

Phoebe Barron, thank you for partnering as the mental health consultant for this message. I could not have written this book without your insight. Renee Tumolo, Vera Holloway, and Melissa Clark, thank you for speaking into this book and sharing your wisdom as mental health professionals.

Jenni Burke, agent extraordinaire, thank you for ten wonderful years of partnership. You are a gift. Carolyn McCready, Carly Kellerman, and the Zondervan team, thank you for your faith in me and my vision for this book since day one.

About the Author

Alli Worthington lives outside Nashville with her husband, Mark, their sons, and a very pampered golden retriever named Eleanor Roosevelt Woofington. Alli loves movies, dairy-free ice cream, and roller coasters.

Alli is an author, speaker, and entrepreneur who spends her days helping women be successful in life and business. She specializes in coaching executives and business owners.

She founded The Coach School to train coaches and help them grow their businesses. She cofounded Called Creatives, which helps women who are called to be writers and speakers get published, get booked to speak, and get connected.

And she loves giving gifts! Alli has a lot of bonuses, gifts, and downloads waiting for you in the following bonus gifts section.

Remaining You
While Raising Them
WORKBOOK

In this free workbook, you'll discover...

- A small group discussion guide
- A guide to tackling the mental load
- A guide for praying for your children
- A guide to breathwork
- Data and research on parenting
- More fun tools to help you thrive

Scan the QR code or visit: alliworthington.com/rywrt-workbook

Also from Alli Worthington...

DOWNLOAD FREE CHAPTERS

Breaking Busy

You have to break the busy before the busy breaks you.

The Year of Living Happy

A devotional that brings practical tools and biblical truth together for greater joy and peace.

Fierce Faith

God didn't give you a spirit of fear; learn how to fight back against it.

Standing Strong

You can't break a woman who draws her strength from God.

SCAN FOR INSTANT ACCESS

Visit alliworthington.com/rywrt-chapters or scan the QR code to get instant access to sample chapters from each of these popular titles!

CALLED CREATIVES

God is doing *BIG* things in the
hearts of women.

IT'S TIME TO ANSWER YOUR CALLING.

Led by bestselling authors, speakers, and industry
experts, Alli Worthington and Lisa Whittle.

Called Creatives is a private coaching community
with hands-on training for writing and speaking
with influence and impact.

www.calledcreatives.com

Notes

Chapter 1: Modern Motherhood Is Broken, and It's Breaking Us

1. "Tired and Stressed, but Satisfied: Moms Juggle Kids, Career and Identity," Barna Group, May 5, 2014, https://www.barna .com/research/tired-stressed-but-satisfied-moms-juggle-kids -career-identity/.

Chapter 2: If Mama Ain't Happy

1. Sara Lane, "Emotional Health vs. Mental Health: The Real Difference," EddinsCounseling.com, December 11, 2020, https:// eddinscounseling.com/emotional-health-vs-mental-health/.

Chapter 3: Your Mom Superpower

1. "'Good Enough' Parenting Is Good Enough, Study Finds," ScienceDaily, May 8, 2019, www.sciencedaily.com/releases /2019/05/190508134511.htm.

Chapter 4: Myth 1: Good Moms Put Their Families First

1. Ashley May, "Study: Parents Spend More Time with Children Now Than They Did 50 Years Ago," *USA Today*, October 1, 2016, https://www.usatoday.com/story/news/nation-now/2016/09/30 /parents-spend-more-time-children-now-than-they-did-50-years -ago/91263880/.
2. Vera Sizensky, "New Survey: Moms Are Putting Their Health

Last," HealthyWomen, March 27, 2015, https://www
.healthywomen.org/content/article/new-survey-moms-are
-putting-their-health-last.

3. "The Science of Sleep: Understanding What Happens When You
   Sleep," Johns Hopkins Medicine, accessed February 1, 2023,
   https://www.hopkinsmedicine.org/health/wellness-and
   -prevention/the-science-of-sleep-understanding-what-happens
   -when-you-sleep.

4. Katherine Harmon, "How Slight Sleep Deprivation Could Add
   Extra Pounds," *Scientific American*, October 24, 2012, https://
   www.scientificamerican.com/article/sleep-deprivation-obesity/.

5. "Study Reveals the Face of Sleep Deprivation," American
   Academy of Sleep Medicine—Association for Sleep Clinicians
   and Researchers, August 30, 2013, https://aasm.org/study
   -reveals-the-face-of-sleep-deprivation/.

6. DeAnn Liska et al., "Narrative Review of Hydration and Selected
   Health Outcomes in the General Population," *Nutrients* 11, no. 1
   (January 1, 2019), https://doi.org/10.3390/nu11010070.

7. Fahimeh Haghighatdoost et al., "Drinking Plain Water Is
   Associated with Decreased Risk of Depression and Anxiety in
   Adults: Results from a Large Cross-Sectional Study," *World Journal
   of Psychiatry* 8, no. 3 (September 20, 2018): 88–96, https://www
   .ncbi.nlm.nih.gov/pmc/articles/PMC6147771/.

8. "Depression and Anxiety: Exercise Eases Symptoms," Mayo
   Clinic, September 27, 2017, https://www.mayoclinic.org/diseases
   -conditions/depression/in-depth/depression-and-exercise/art
   -20046495.

9. Ying Chen and Tyler J. VanderWeele, "Associations of Religious
   Upbringing with Subsequent Health and Well-Being from
   Adolescence to Young Adulthood: An Outcome-Wide Analysis,"
   American Journal of Epidemiology 187, no. 11 (November 2018):
   2355–64, https://academic.oup.com/aje/article/187/11
   /2355/5094534.

10. William Collinge and Paul Yarnold, "Transformational Breath

Work in Medical Illness: Clinical Application and Evidence of Immunoenhancement," *Subtle Energies and Energy Medicine* 12, no. 3 (2001): 139–56, https://journals.sfu.ca/seemj/index.php /seemj/article/viewFile/326/288; Tanja Miller and Laila Nielsen, "Measure of Significance of Holotropic Breathwork in the Development of Self-Awareness," *Journal of Alternative and Complementary Medicine* 21, no. 12 (December 2015): 796–803, https://pubmed.ncbi.nlm.nih.gov/26565611/.

11. *This Is Us*, season 5, episode 12, "Both Things Can Be True," written and produced by K. J. Steinberg, aired April 6, 2021, on NBC.

Chapter 5: Myth 2: Good Moms' Kids Are Obedient and Well-Behaved

1. Faye Elkins, "Animal Cruelty: A Serious Crime Leading to Horrific Outcomes," *Community Policing Dispatch* 12, no. 3 (April 2019), https://cops.usdoj.gov/html/dispatch/04-2019 /animal_cruelty.html.
2. Proverbs 22:6.
3. Simone Marie Scully, "What Are Enmeshed Relationships? And How to Set Boundaries," Psych Central, July 30, 2021, https:// psychcentral.com/lib/tips-on-setting-boundaries-in-enmeshed -relationships#what-are-they.

Chapter 6: Myth 3: Good Moms Don't Get Angry

1. Rusty Fleischer and Jerry Medol, "Fight or Flight: The Physiological Response," Anger Alternatives, accessed July 13, 2022, https://www.anger.org/healthy-anger/fight-or-flight-the -physiological-response.html.
2. Ephesians 4:26–27 NIV.

Chapter 7: Myth 4: Good Moms Protect Their Children from Pain

1. Patrick A. Coleman, "The Strange Reason Tummy Time Was Invented for Babies," Fatherly, November 9, 2017, https://www .fatherly.com/health-science/tummy-time-reasons.

2. "Anxiety Is the Top Mental Health Issue for College Students," Boston Evening Therapy Associates, November 4, 2015, https://bostoneveningtherapy.com/anxiety-surpasses-depression-as-most-common-college-mental-health-issue/.

3. Alison Escalante, "The Parenting 'Shouldstorm'," TEDx Talks, November 29, 2018, YouTube video, 16:42, https://www.youtube.com/watch?v=mYT7EDi_nOs.

Chapter 8: Myth 5: Good Moms Can Do It All

1. Sarah Aswell, "The 'Encanto' Song That Sums Up How I Feel about Being a Mom Right Now," Scary Mommy, February 3, 2022, https://www.scarymommy.com/the-encanto-song-surface-pressure-moms.

2. Alison Escalante, "The Parenting 'Shouldstorm'," TEDx Talks, November 29, 2018, YouTube video, 16:42, https://www.youtube.com/watch?v=mYT7EDi_nOs.

3. Alison Escalante, "The Parenting 'Shouldstorm'."

4. Claire McCarthy, "Anxiety in Teens Is Rising: What's Going On?" HealthyChildren.org, November 20, 2019, https://www.healthychildren.org/English/health-issues/conditions/emotional-problems/Pages/Anxiety-Disorders.aspx.

5. Erin Eatough, "What Is Mental Load? Recognize the Burden of Invisible Labor," *BetterUp* (blog), January 4, 2022, https://www.betterup.com/blog/mental-load.

6. Edwin Chen, "Twins Reared Apart: A Living Lab," *New York Times*, December 9, 1979, https://www.nytimes.com/1979/12/09/archives/twins-reared-apart-a-living-lab.html.

7. Seth Stephens-Davidowitz, "The One Parenting Decision That Really Matters," *Atlantic*, May 23, 2022, https://www.theatlantic.com/ideas/archive/2022/05/parenting-decisions-dont-trust-your-gut-book-excerpt/629734/.

8. Michael S. Kramer et al., "Effects of Prolonged and Exclusive Breastfeeding on Child Height, Weight, Adiposity, and Blood Pressure at Age 6.5 Y: Evidence from a Large Randomized Trial,"

American Journal of Clinical Nutrition 86, no. 6 (December 1, 2007): 1717–21, https://academic.oup.com/ajcn/article/86/6/1717/5064857.

9. Matthew Gentzkow and Jesse M. Shapiro, "Preschool Television Viewing and Adolescent Test Scores: Historical Evidence from the Coleman Study," *Quarterly Journal of Economics* (February 2008): https://scholar.harvard.edu/files/shapiro/files/tv.pdf.

10. Mary Sawtell, "Does Teaching Children How to Play Cognitively Demanding Games Improve Their Educational Attainment? Evidence from a Randomised Controlled Trial of Chess Instruction in England," UCL Institute of Education (February 2017): https://www.academia.edu/53638211/Does_teaching_children_how_to_play_cognitively_demanding_games_improve_their_educational_attainment_Evidence_from_a_Randomised_Controlled_Trial_of_chess_instruction_in_England.

11. Emily Oster, *The Family Firm: A Data-Driven Guide to Better Decision Making in the Early School Years* (New York: Penguin, 2021).

Chapter 9: Small Changes, Big Results

1. William J. Chopik, "Associations among Relational Values, Support, Health, and Well-Being across the Adult Lifespan," *Personal Relationships* 24, no. 2 (June 2017): 408–22, https://doi.org/10.1111/pere.12187.

2. James Clear, *Atomic Habits: Tiny Changes, Remarkable Results: An Easy & Proven Way to Build Good Habits & Break Bad Ones* (New York: Random House, 2018), 22.

Chapter 10: The Magic Question Habit

1. Doris Baumann and Willibald Ruch, "Measuring What Counts in Life: The Development and Initial Validation of the Fulfilled Life Scale (FLS)," *Frontiers in Psychology* 12 (January 2021), https://doi.org/10.3389/fpsyg.2021.795931.

2. Philippians 4:19 NIV.

Chapter 11: The Power of a Great Soundtrack

1. "The Teen Brain: 7 Things to Know," National Institute of Mental Health, retrieved June 28, 2022, https://www.nimh.nih.gov/health/publications/the-teen-brain-7-things-to-know#.

Chapter 12: Getting the Love You Need

1. Mark Johnson, "Why Having Children Is Bad for Your Marriage," *Washington Post*, May 6, 2016, https://www.washingtonpost.com/posteverything/wp/2016/05/06/why-having-children-is-bad-for-your-marriage/.

2. Thomas Hansen, "Parenthood and Happiness: A Review of Folk Theories versus Empirical Evidence," *Social Indicators Research* 108 (2012): 29–64, https://link.springer.com/article/10.1007/s11205-011-9865-y.

3. John M. Gottman and Nan Silver, *The Seven Principles for Making Marriage Work: A Practical Guide from the International Bestselling Relationship Expert* (UK: Orion Spring, 2018), 169.

4. John M. Gottman and Nan Silver, *Why Marriages Succeed or Fail: And How You Can Make Your Marriage Last* (New York: Simon & Schuster, 1995), 73.

5. Gottman and Silver, *Why Marriages Succeed or Fail*, 58.

6. Eric Barker, *Plays Well with Others: The Surprising Science behind Why Everything You Know about Relationships Is (Mostly) Wrong* (New York: HarperOne, 2022), 153.

7. John M. Gottman and Sybil Carrère, "Predicting Divorce among Newlyweds from the First Three Minutes of a Marital Conflict Discussion," *Family Process* 38, no. 3 (September 1999): 293–301, https://doi.org/10.1111/j.1545-5300.1999.00293.x.

8. Gottman and Silver, *Why Marriages Succeed or Fail*, 58.

9. Kyle Benson, "The Magic Relationship Ratio, According to Science," Gottman Institute, retrieved August 8, 2022, https://www.gottman.com/blog/the-magic-relationship-ratio-according-science/.

10. Gary Chapman, *The 5 Love Languages: The Secret to Love That Lasts* (Chicago: Northfield, 2017).

11. Rachel Van Wickle, "Couples Communication: Assuming Positive Intentions," *Covenant Family Solutions* (blog), July 8, 2021, https://covenantfamilysolutions.com/blog/couples-communication-assuming-positive-intentions/.

12. K. Bridbord, "Assuming Positive Intent Is a Relationship Superpower—Here's Why," Founders Foundry, September 27, 2020, https://thefoundersfoundry.com/articles/assuming-positive-intent-is-a-relationship-superpowerheres-why.

13. Brené Brown, *Daring Greatly: How the Courage to Be Vulnerable Transforms the Way We Live, Love, Parent, and Lead* (New York: Penguin Random House, 2017), 45.

Chapter 13: The Secret Sauce in the Happiness Recipe

1. 1 Corinthians 13:4–5 NIV.

2. Gary Thomas, *When to Walk Away: Finding Freedom from Toxic People* (Grand Rapids: Zondervan, 2019), 55.

3. Eric Barker, "How to Have Great Relationships with Eric Barker, Episode 213," May 23, 2022, in *The Alli Worthington Show*, podcast, https://alliworthington.com/ericbarker/.

4. William J. Chopik, "Associations among Relational Values, Support, Health, and Well-Being across the Adult Lifespan," *Personal Relationships* 24, no. 2 (June 2017): 408–22, https://doi.org/10.1111/pere.12187.

5. Eun Kyong Shin et al., "Association of Maternal Social Relationships with Cognitive Development in Early Childhood," *JAMA Network Open* 2, no. 1 (2019): e186963, https://doi.org/10.1001/jamanetworkopen.2018.6963.

6. Kyong Shin, "Association of Maternal Social Relationships."

7. Lisa Rapaport, "Mother's Friendships May Be Good for Babies' Brains," Reuters, February 1, 2019, https://www.reuters.com/article/us-health-children-social-mothers/mothers-friendships-may-be-good-for-babies-brains-idUSKCN1PQ5NI.

8. "Loneliness in America," Cigna, retrieved June 21, 2022, https://newsroom.cigna.com/loneliness-in-america.

9. "Bert N. Uchino, Ph.D.," University of Utah, retrieved June 21, 2022, https://psych.utah.edu/people/faculty/uchino-bert.php.

10. "Loneliness and Social Isolation Linked to Serious Health Conditions," Centers for Disease Control and Prevention, April 29, 2021, https://www.cdc.gov/aging/publications/features/lonely-older-adults.html.

11. Elena Renken, "Most Americans Are Lonely, and Our Workplace Culture May Not Be Helping," NPR, January 23, 2020, https://www.npr.org/sections/health-shots/2020/01/23/798676465/most-americans-are-lonely-and-our-workplace-culture-may-not-be-helping.

12. "It's Not If, but How People Use Social Media That Impacts Their Well-Being," ScienceDaily, November 2, 2020, https://www.sciencedaily.com/releases/2020/11/201102110030.html.

13. Nedra Glover Tawwab, *Set Boundaries, Find Peace: A Guide to Reclaiming Yourself* (New York: TarcherPerigee, 2021), 5.

Chapter 14: The Secret Art of Confident Motherhood

1. Naomi Stadlen, quoted in Flannery Dean, "To Mother or to Parent: Is There a Difference?," Chatelaine, September 13, 2011, https://chatelaine.com/living/to-mother-or-to-parent-is-there-a-difference/.

From the Publisher

GREAT BOOKS

ARE EVEN BETTER WHEN THEY'RE SHARED!

Help other readers find this one:

- Post a review at your favorite online bookseller

- Post a picture on a social media account and share why you enjoyed it

- Send a note to a friend who would also love it—or better yet, give them a copy

Thanks for reading!